CONQUERING
INFERTILITY

CONQUERING INFERTILITY

MEDICAL CHALLENGES AND MORAL DILEMMAS

Elizabeth L. Marshall

The Changing Family

Franklin Watts
A Division of Grolier Publishing
New York • London • Hong Kong • Sydney
Danbury, Connecticut

For Jeff, Abigail,

and Amanda

Photographs ©: AP/Wide Workd Photos: 107; Archive Photos: 56 Peter Arnold Inc.:
22, 40, 74–75, 97 (SIU); Reuters/Corbis-Bettman: 91
Illustrations by Vantage Art

Library of Congress Cataloging-in-Publication Data

Marshall, Elizabeth L.
    Conquering infertility: medical challenges and moral dilemmas/ by
    Elizabeth L. Marshall
    p.   cm. —(The Changing Family)
    Includes bibliographical references and index.
    Summary: Discusses the causes of infertility, making the decision to seek
treatment, various treatment methods, and controversies surrounding them.
    ISBN 0-531-11344-2
    1. Human reproductive technology—Juvenile literature. 2. Human reproductive
technology—Moral and ethical aspects—Juvenile literature. 3. Infertility—Juvenile
literature. [1. Infertility. 2. Human reproduction.] I. Title. II. Series: Changing family
(New York, NY)
RG133.5.M38   1997
616.6'92—dc21

                96-39440
                CIP
                AC

CONTENTS

ACKNOWLEDGMENTS

Many thanks to Helen and Dave Krouse, Lisa and John Veerlos, and Carole and Paul White from the Columbus site for RESOLVE of Ohio. Your willingness to share your thoughts and feelings as you coped with infertility was greatly appreciated.

Thank you to Seth D. Feltheimer, M.D., of the College of Physicians & Surgeons of Columbia University for commenting on a draft of this manuscript.

CONQUERING
INFERTILITY

INTRODUCTION

On July 25, 1978, the birth announcement of Louise Brown electrified the world. Louise was the first human ever born who was conceived by *in vitro fertilization (IVF)*. At a laboratory in Oldham, England, medical scientists combined an *egg* from Lesley Brown with *sperm* from her husband, John Brown. Two-and-a-half days later, the *fertilized egg* was transferred to Lesley's *uterus* where the pregnancy progressed like any other. When Louise Brown was born, the press quickly dubbed her a "test-tube baby" and pictures of her were splashed around the world.

The first American in vitro baby, Elizabeth Carr, was born in 1981. Since then, in vitro fertilization has lead to more than 30,000 births in the United States. The last two decades have seen an explosion of new developments in fertility medicine. The most dramatic of these techniques are based on conception outside the body.

Today, about 300 fertility clinics perform in vitro fertilization in the United States. By using this technique, couples with a wide range of fertility problems are able to have a child. It is even possible for women who lack healthy eggs to achieve pregnancy by using eggs from donors. In addition, a woman without a healthy womb can become a mother by having an *embryo* created with her own egg implanted in another woman.

Other new procedures have also brought hope to thousands of infertile couples. Medical scientists have found a way to inject a single sperm into an egg, thereby making it possible for some infertile men to father children. Fertility experts can also help sperm find their way into the egg by cutting a small hole in the egg's outer layer.

Fertility medicine is not all high-tech laboratory procedures, however. Use of *fertility drugs* or surgery has also helped many couples become parents. Indeed, most couples who have trouble conceiving naturally are helped by such conventional treatments. Very few people resort to in vitro fertilization.

The American Society for Reproductive Medicine (ASRM) estimates that, in the United States, 2.6 million couples are currently having trouble conceiving a child. This is a significant portion of the population. Perhaps that is why *infertility* attracts quite a bit of media attention.

This figure may be higher than it was a decade or two ago because many members of the baby boom generation—that enormous group of people born between 1946 and 1964—married later and started their families later than their parents and grandparents. The number of women over age 35 giving birth to their first baby has more than doubled in recent years.

A woman is most fertile between ages 15 and 24. As she ages, it becomes more and more difficult for her to become pregnant. That is one reason why a higher percentage of baby boomers have faced fertility problems.

In addition, several medical studies have suggested that male infertility is increasing because of the widespread use of certain kinds of chemicals that affect the action of human hormones.

Infertility is also in the news because its treatment raises serious ethical questions, not only for the couples involved but for society as a whole. Fertility treatment can be very expensive. A month's worth of powerful fertility drugs can cost more than $1,000. One attempt at in vitro fertilization averages $6,000 or $7,000. Fertility treatment is usually not covered by health insurance. Should it be? Some states have passed legislation requiring its coverage.

Fertility treatment can be physically uncomfortable and sometimes painful. One study has identified a link between the long-term use of fertility drugs and cancer. Almost all couples find treatment emotionally stressful. It also carries no guarantees of success. But when should a couple stop treatment? When does treatment no longer carry any hope? And can couples truly be said to give their informed consent to a procedure if its long-term effects are unknown?

Another significant side effect of fertility treatment is the risk of *multiple births*. Most births are twins, but the rate of triplets, quadruplets, and more has sky rocketed in recent years. Multiple births may result from the use of fertility drugs or high-tech procedures like in vitro fertilization. Giving birth to multiples puts a tremendous strain on the parents, as well as on society's resources.

Despite these important concerns, it's safe to say that the main reason infertility has captured the headlines is because of the stunning advances made possible by high-tech procedures. Technologies like in vitro fertilization catch our attention because they strike at the very heart of the creation of life. They seem to imply that Mother Nature must now share the stage with science. They evoke images of Frankenstein or the futuristic novel *Brave New World*. The technological possibilities are exciting—but also frightening.

Few people would deny the pain and disappointment felt by couples who are unsuccessful in their efforts to achieve pregnancy. But the idea of using laboratory procedures to fertilize a human egg is abhorrent to some people. The Roman Catholic Church has condemned *assisted reproductive technology*.

In vitro fertilization also raises troubling issues for many people on grounds other than religious beliefs. What if a physician or a technician makes a mistake during in vitro fertilization? What if the wrong egg is fertilized by the wrong sperm? The result is the conception of a person who was never meant to be. Although fertility specialists emphasize that this is extraordinarily unlikely, it has happened.

In 1995, a Dutch woman who had several embryos implanted in her uterus gave birth to twins with different fathers. Even more chilling than mistakes is intentional fraud. State authorities recently accused the director of a fertility clinic in Irvine, California, of deliberately removing eggs from some patients, fertilizing them, and implanting the eggs in other patients.

These headlines startle and amaze us. In 1991, a South Dakota woman carried twins conceived with eggs from her daughter and sperm from her son-in-law. She did it to help her daughter, who was born without a uterus. In Britain, a 59-year-old woman recently gave birth to twins. This sparked a debate on both sides of the Atlantic about whether women in their 50s should become new mothers.

Even as we applaud the science, we are made uneasy by how the world is changing. Is it natural? Is it right? Does the opportunity to help infertile couples outweigh the risks? Different countries have answered these questions in different ways. Germany and Switzerland are among the nations, for instance, that have banned egg donation outright.

This book describes the causes of infertility and how young people can protect their fertility. It also reviews the conventional medical therapies that can be used to achieve conception, and looks at the history of in vitro fertilization and its variations. The last portion of the book outlines the criticisms that have been lobbed at the fertility industry and how the industry has responded. It also describes the end of fertility treatment, particularly the hard decisions faced by couples who have not achieved pregnancy.

1

THE

CAUSES

OF

INFERTILITY

Infertility is unlike other medical problems. People who are infertile often look and feel perfectly healthy. It is very likely that they don't even know they have a problem until they try to conceive a baby. A couple may be married for several years before beginning to suspect they have a fertility problem.

Doctors define infertility as the failure to conceive a baby after 1 year of regular sexual intercourse without birth control. About 1 in 10 couples who try to conceive have trouble getting pregnant, according to the American Society for Reproductive Medicine. Approximately 2.6 million couples in the United States are affected by infertility.

Although infertility was traditionally thought to be caused by a problem with the woman's reproductive ability, modern medicine has shown that such a judgment was based on sexism, not science. Both men and women can have fertility problems. In 40 percent of infertile couples, the problem is with the woman's reproductive system. In another 40 percent, the problem is with the man's reproductive system.

It is not uncommon for several factors to cause infertility in a couple.

Sometimes, no specific problem can be found in couples who are unable to conceive. In about 20 percent of couples, the diagnosis is *unexplained infertility*. This conclusion is very frustrating because there is not enough information to guide the couple and their physician toward the best form of medical treatment. As a result, couples may undergo a variety of treatments before finding one that works.

Another kind of infertility can occur when a woman is able to get pregnant, but can't stay pregnant. She may be able to conceive, but some hormonal or physical abnormality prevents the *fetus* from developing properly. The fetus usually dies during early pregnancy. The woman passes some blood, as with a *menstrual period*, and may have painful cramps. In many cases, the fetus is expelled with the blood. This is known as a *miscarriage*.

Miscarriages are not uncommon. Most are the result of genetic abnormalities in the fetus. Many women with healthy children have had at least one miscarriage. However, a woman who suffers repeated miscarriages, without ever carrying a pregnancy the full 9 months, has a medical problem. She, too, is counted among the infertile.

Infertility may strike those who least expect it. For example, a man and woman who have had one child together may have great difficulty conceiving a second child. In such cases, reproductive problems, such as *endometriosis* or pelvic infection, may have occurred since the couple's first baby was born. This, too, is considered a fertility problem and is referred to as *secondary infertility*.

Human Reproduction: How it Works

For a human egg to be successfully fertilized by a human sperm, many carefully timed steps must occur. Any interference with this sequence—whether due to disease, faulty hormones, or poor timing—can prevent conception. Getting

FEMALE REPRODUCTIVE SYSTEM

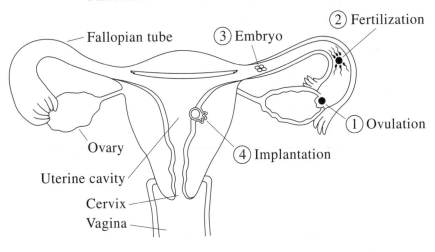

1. *Each month, one ovary releases an egg into the fallopian tube.*
2. *If the egg comes into contact with sperm, fertilization may occur.*
3. *As a fertilized egg continues to travel toward the uterus, it divides several times. At this point, it is called an embryo.*
4. *About 14 days after conception, the embryo attaches itself in the uterine lining, where it will grow and develop for about 9 months.*

pregnant is not simple! In fact, it's complicated enough that anyone who studies this area marvels that any couple at all is able to conceive a baby. In any given month, a healthy fertile couple has about a 20 percent chance of conception. Over a period of 1 year, however, about 85 percent will achieve pregnancy.

Conception is possible for only a few days during a woman's monthly menstrual cycle. By puberty, a woman has about 400,000 immature eggs inside her two *ovaries*. Each ovary is located very near a *fallopian tube* that leads to the uterus. At the beginning of each cycle, one egg matures inside a *follicle* within the ovary.

At mid-cycle, roughly day 14 of the average 28-day cycle, the egg is released from its follicle and swept into a fallopian tube. This is known as *ovulation*. The ovary that releases the egg alternates from month to month—one month it is the left ovary; the next month it is the right.

Pinpointing the time of ovulation is extremely important for couples trying to achieve pregnancy. After ovulation, the egg must encounter sperm within 12 to 24 hours for *fertilization* to occur. However, that doesn't necessarily mean sexual intercourse must take place during those brief hours.

Sperm can live in the female reproductive tract for several days, so intercourse that takes place 2 or 3 days before ovulation can still cause pregnancy. In addition, some women may produce eggs that remain fertile longer than 24 hours, in which case intercourse that takes place 1 or 2 days after ovulation can also result in pregnancy. Couples with impaired fertility often try to time intercourse precisely with ovulation to increase their chances of conception.

Immediately after ovulation, the egg travels the length of the fallopian tube toward the uterus. In preparation for the arrival of a fertilized egg, the lining of the uterus thickens with blood and nutrients. If fertilization has occurred, the fertilized egg will consist of four or eight cells by the time it enters the uterus. At this stage, the fertilized egg is more properly known as a *zygote* or embryo.

After about 14 days in the uterus, the embryo attaches itself to the uterine lining in a process called *implantation*. If fertilization has not occurred, the lining of the uterus is sloughed off and expelled during the woman's period. After all the material is removed and menstrual bleeding stops, a new menstrual cycle begins.

The body manufactures substances known as hormones that are responsible for the smooth running of the menstrual cycle. The egg is stimulated to mature inside a follicle by a hormone called, simply enough, *follicle-stimulating hor-*

mone. Luteinizing hormone, which is produced by the *pituitary gland*, prompts the release of the egg from the follicle. The ruptured follicle then secretes *estrogen* and *progesterone*, the two hormones that signal the uterine lining to prepare for possible implantation of a fertilized egg. The *thyroid gland* also produces hormones that are important for reproduction.

The Sperm's Role

Although millions of sperm—200 million to 500 million— are present when a healthy man *ejaculates*, fewer than 200 actually reach the egg in the fallopian tube and only one can fertilize it. For this reason, only the strongest and healthiest sperm have even a chance of fertilizing an egg. Fertilization occurs when the first sperm successfully penetrates the outer layer of the egg, known as the *zona pellucida*.

Sperm are produced in the *testicles*. The testicles hang outside the male body, in the *scrotum*, and are maintained at a temperature of 94°F (34°C), slightly below normal body temperature. When the sperm are fully mature, they travel through the *sperm ducts* toward the *urethra*. Along the way the sperm combine with fluids produced by several glands, including the *prostate gland*. The mix of fluids and sperm is called *semen*. Semen is released through the urethral opening at the tip of the penis during ejaculation. (So is urine, although never at the same time as semen.) If a man's sperm are damaged by illness or exposure to a toxin, he can expect to have healthy sperm again in 72 days.

Ninety-eight percent of the male ejaculate consists of thick fluids; the other 2 percent is the tadpole-shaped sperm cells. During intercourse, the semen is deposited in the woman's *vagina*. From there, the sperm must actively swim through the *cervix* and uterus to reach the fallopian tubes in their quest to fertilize an egg.

During ovulation, the mucus present in the cervix changes in a way that makes it easier for the sperm to pass

MALE REPRODUCTIVE SYSTEM

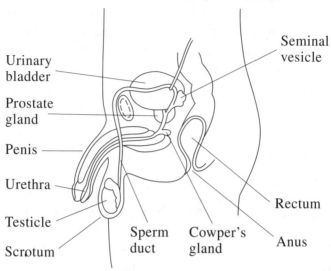

Sperm are produced in the testicles. When they are mature, the sperm travel through the sperm ducts and mix with fluids produced in the prostate and Cowper's glands. During sexual intercourse, this mixture—called semen—flows into the penis and is released into a woman's vagina.

through. Nevertheless, the journey is still difficult and only the strongest and most active sperm reach the tubes. The reason that many millions of sperm start the journey is to guarantee that at least a few will survive to finish it. Men with low sperm counts often have fertility problems—so do men with sluggish or abnormally shaped sperm or those whose ejaculate has less than normal volume.

The Peak of Fertility

Young women have babies; old women do not. Even small children know this. As a woman approaches age 45, her ovaries stop releasing eggs regularly and the eggs she does release often fertilize and implant less easily. By her late 40s or early 50s, a woman stops ovulating and menstruating altogether. This process, known as *menopause*, occurs gradually.

But how old is too old to get pregnant? That varies greatly from individual to individual. On average, however, fertility drops steeply after age 35 when about 1 in 5 women have trouble conceiving. After age 40, about half of all women have problems conceiving. Age may be the only factor impairing a couple's ability to conceive or it may be one of several factors. It's an important factor, however. A couple in which the woman is age 35 or older may seek medical help for infertility earlier than a couple in which the woman is younger.

The couple may elect to start fertility treatment with a physician after 6 months of failing to conceive, rather than 12 months. They know that medical treatment is less effective as a woman grows older and that female fertility drops off swiftly after age 40. For this reason, fertility clinics typically separate their success rates into two categories: one for women under age 40 and one for women age 40 and older.

Infertility in Women

Some common causes of female infertility include ovulatory disorders, abnormal hormone levels, premature menopause, endometriosis, blocked or missing fallopian tubes, uterine disorders, and *cervical mucus incompatibility*.

Ovulatory Disorders

Ovulatory disorders account for about 25 percent of female infertility. Women who ovulate too early or too late during their menstrual cycle may have impaired fertility. Women who ovulate infrequently are producing few eggs and, therefore, have fewer opportunities to become pregnant. Women who are extremely thin or overweight may also have problems ovulating. So may athletes who have very little body fat.

HOW TO PREVENT INFERTILITY

Many factors can cause infertility. Some are not in your control. But some are, even if you're only a teenager now and don't plan to have children for years. There are a number of ways to protect yourself right now from becoming infertile.

Protect yourself from sexually transmitted diseases (STDs).

The American Society for Reproductive Medicine estimates that one-fourth of all cases of infertility are the result of *a sexually transmitted disease*. The United States has the highest rate of STDs of any developed country in the world.[1] An estimated 12 million new cases of STDs occur each year in the United States; two-thirds occur in people under age 25.

The only certain way to avoid STDs is *abstinence*. If you are sexually active, limit your number of partners and use a condom every single time you have sex. Your risk of contracting a STD is lower if your relationship is *monogamous*.

Get tested if you think you may have been exposed to a STD. *Chlamydia* and *gonorrhea* can be treated with antibiotics. If caught early, you can prevent pelvic inflammatory disease from developing. The ASRM has called pelvic inflammatory disease the most common preventable cause of infertility in the United States.

Kick the habit and get healthy.

Smoking is bad for your heart and lungs. Excessive drinking will play havoc with your health. Street drugs, like cocaine and marijuana, are illegal and bad for your body. If those risks aren't enough, medical studies have also linked cigarette smoke, alcohol, and drugs to impaired fertility.

Avoid exposure to radiation and environmental toxins.

Exposure to high levels of lead, mercury, ethylene oxide, and pesticides may reduce fertility. Working with cars, paints and varnishes, or building materials may bring you into contact with some of these toxins. Certain substances found in paper manufacturing have also been associated with reproductive problems.

Sometimes the underlying cause of irregular or infrequent ovulation can be identified. It is possible that the woman's thyroid or pituitary gland is malfunctioning. Or she may have *polycystic ovarian disease*, which occurs when the ovaries fail to ovulate and form tiny cysts instead.

Even though it is not always possible to pinpoint the cause of ovulatory disorders, such conditions can very often be treated successfully with fertility drugs.

Abnormal Hormone Levels

A variety of hormone problems can interfere with conception and pregnancy. Recurrent miscarriage, in some cases, may occur because the body is unable to produce enough of the right hormones to maintain pregnancy. Recurrent miscarriage can sometimes be prevented with drug treatment.

Premature Menopause

A complete absence of ovulation and menstruation in a young woman is known as premature menopause. Unfortunately, the production of eggs cannot be stimulated in a woman who has undergone premature menopause. Such women must rely on adoption or *donor eggs*—eggs taken from the ovaries of a fertile woman and donated to an infertile woman.

Endometriosis

Endometriosis is a poorly-understood disease that occurs when tissue from the lining of the uterus grows on the ovaries and other pelvic organs. The tissue can be thin and web-like or very dense. Symptoms range from heavy, painful periods to no symptoms at all. The link between endometriosis and infertility is hotly debated by physicians. The disease is present in about 35 percent of women with fertility problems. This is frequent enough to suggest some sort of connection. It may be that the overgrowth of tissue interferes with the ability of the egg to travel from the ovary to the fallopian tube. The growth of endometriosis can be

23

treated with drugs or surgery with the hope that fertility will improve when the disease is reduced.

Blocked or Missing Fallopian Tubes

A blocked or absent fallopian tube prevents the egg from meeting the sperm. If only one tube is blocked, fertilization is possible every other month in the unblocked tube. Scar tissue from *pelvic inflammatory disease*—an infection in the uterus, tubes, and pelvis—can cause blocked or misshapen fallopian tubes. Tubal blockage accounts for about 35 percent of fertility problems in women.

Sexually transmitted diseases, such as chlamydia and gonorrhea, can cause pelvic inflammatory disease. Sexual intercourse with an affected partner introduces organisms that infect the cervix, uterus, tubes, and other parts of the pelvis, if left untreated. Unfortunately, women infected with chlamydia or gonorrhea often have no symptoms and fail to seek treatment with antibiotics. Pelvic infection can also be caused by an *intrauterine device (IUD)*, which is used to prevent pregnancy. The Dalkon Shield, one type of IUD, was taken off the market for this reason.

A woman with scarred tubes is also at risk for an *ectopic pregnancy*, a situation that occurs when a fertilized egg grows in the fallopian tube rather than the uterus. If an ectopic pregnancy goes unnoticed, it can be life-threatening. It will cause the fallopian tube to rupture, resulting in massive internal bleeding. To prevent tubal rupture, an ectopic pregnancy must be promptly ended with surgery.

Before the success of in vitro fertilization, the only way to restore fertility to women with blocked tubes was with corrective surgery. But in many cases, unfortunately, the tubes are too badly damaged for surgery to be successful. In vitro fertilization was developed to give women with blocked or missing fallopian tubes a chance at becoming pregnant. In fact, the rise of in vitro fertilization has reduced the number of tubal surgeries by 50 percent.

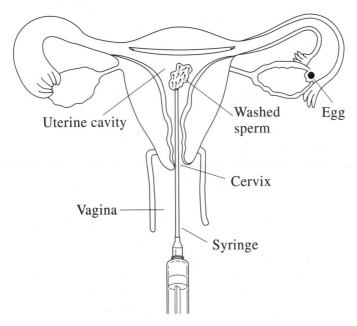

In intrauterine insemination, a syringe containing sperm is inserted into the uterus.

Cervical Mucus Incompatibility

During most of a woman's menstrual cycle, the mucus in her cervix is thick and acidic. The mucus creates an environment unfriendly to bacteria and, to some extent, sperm. Around ovulation, however, the cervical mucus becomes thin, stretchy, and hospitable to sperm. In some women, the mucus normally fails to change and remains unfriendly to sperm. This condition is known as cervical mucus incompatibility.

Doctors disagree about the extent to which cervical mucus incompatibility contributes to infertility. Some physicians, however, recommend a procedure known as *intrauterine insemination or assisted insemination.* In this simple procedure, the man contributes sperm through masterbation. Then, the sperm are placed directly into a woman's uterus. As a result, the sperm do not have to fight their way through the cervix and vagina.

Uterine Disorders

Just as it's important for the fallopian tubes to function properly, so must the uterus offer a safe home for a fertilized egg. A uterus that is irregularly shaped or filled with cysts may not allow a fertilized egg to implant. Even if the egg is able to implant, problems with the shape or size of the uterus may prevent the developing embryo from growing, and lead to miscarriage.

Uterine abnormalities in some women can be traced to the prescription of a drug known as *diethylstilbestrol* (*DES*). This drug was given to pregnant women between 1940 and 1971 to prevent miscarriage. The daughters of some of the women who took DES during pregnancy suffer from structural defects in the uterus, fallopian tubes, or cervix. DES daughters also have a higher than normal rate of vaginal and cervical cancer.

Infertility in Men

Research into the causes of male infertility is a relatively new field. As a result, far less is known about the causes of male infertility than about the causes of female infertility, and fewer successful treatments are available for male infertility than female infertility.

For this reason, fertility clinics describing the success of their programs may divide their patients into two groups: those with male infertility as a factor and those without. Some experts predict that research in male infertility will make tremendous strides in the next 20 years. The most common causes of male infertility include low sperm count or unhealthy sperm, sperm duct blockages, *varicoceles*, and *male impotence*.

Low Sperm Count or Unhealthy Sperm

Sperm must meet several criteria to be considered normal and capable of fertilizing an egg. A normal sperm count is 20 million to 100 million sperm per milliliter of semen. At least 50 percent of the sperm should be able to swim forward and 50 to 60 percent should have a normal form. The volume of the ejaculate should be 2 to 5 milliliters or more. Men whose semen fails to meet these standards are considered to have a fertility problem.

Sperm abnormalities may be the result of a hormonal imbalance or a structural defect in the male reproductive organs. A lack of healthy sperm can sometimes be linked to diseases, such as diabetes or adolescent mumps.

Some lifestyle factors can temporarily decrease sperm production. Drugs, including prescription medications, illegal drugs like marijuana and cocaine, and anabolic steroids can reduce sperm count. So can infections in the sex glands, fevers, workplace toxins, alcohol, and smoking. Men who frequently use hot tubs or saunas may also inadvertently decrease their sperm production by exposing their testicles to too much heat. Wearing boxer shorts, however, rather than tighter-fitting jockeys has not been scientifically proven to make a difference in testicular temperature.

Several recent studies have also concluded that sperm counts worldwide are falling due to the widespread use of chemicals known as *endocrine disruptors*. Endocrine disruptors are everywhere—in plastics, pesticides, shampoos, cosmetics, and other household products. They are human-made chemicals that mimic natural hormones. One major investigation, conducted by a Danish team led by Niels Skakkebaek and published in the *British Medical Journal* in September 1992, charted a decline in sperm counts worldwide during the past 50 years.[2] Not all medical scientists agree with the conclusions of such studies. Still, there is mounting evidence that such chemicals may be responsible for some cases of infertility, particularly unexplained male infertility.

Because so many factors can affect sperm count, it is often difficult to determine the cause of an individual's low sperm count. As a result, many such cases go unexplained.

Sperm Duct Blockage

About 15 percent of infertile men are diagnosed with sperm duct blockage. Blockages in the sperm ducts prevent sperm from reaching the urethra. Some sperm duct conditions can be cured with surgery.

Many men who wish to have no more children undergo an operation in which their sperm ducts are intentionally cut. This procedure, which is the most popular form of birth control in the United States, is called a *vasectomy*. Men who undergo a vasectomy sometimes decide later that they would like to father more children, perhaps in a second marriage. These men are counted among the infertile. (In some cases, it is possible to reverse a vasectomy.)

Varicocele

A varicose vein in a testicle can cause an increase in the temperature of the scrotum and, perhaps, a reduction in sperm production. Varicoceles are fairly common in all men, however, not just those with fertility problems. Some doctors believe they contribute slightly to infertility since about 25 to 30 percent of infertile men have a varicocele, as compared to just 10 to 15 percent of fertile men. A varicocele can be treated with surgery.

Male Impotence

In rare situations, infertility is caused by male impotence. A man who is impotent has a healthy reproductive system and is producing normal sperm, but he is unable to maintain an *erection* during intercourse. For whatever reason, he cannot transfer his sperm to the woman's vagina.

Other Causes of Infertility

Infertility may be the result of a combination of male and female factors. It can also be caused by outside circumstances that affect the couple together. Some additional causes of infertility include ill-timed intercourse, immune system dysfunction, and physical or mental stress.

Ill-timed Intercourse

If a couple is engaging in regular intercourse, two or three times a week, they are quite likely to have intercourse during ovulation. Identifying ovulation becomes important for couples whose schedules fail to allow for frequent intercourse. To achieve pregnancy, these couples may have to postpone business trips or change other plans so they can be together during ovulation.

Timing is also critical for women with longer than normal menstrual cycles—cycles that last 35 days for instance. Since they ovulate only once every 35 days, they have fewer opportunities to become pregnant than women with shorter cycles. Irregular menstrual cycles are another problem. Women with irregular cycles may find it difficult to predict when they are likely to ovulate and thus miss opportunities to become pregnant.

Women can observe changes in their body temperature and vaginal mucus to determine when ovulation has occurred. Ovulation predictor kits are also available at drugstores.

Immune System Dysfunction

Ordinarily, antibodies produced by the immune system attack foreign substances in the body. During reproduction, however, the woman's immune system must treat sperm—and later, the embryo—kindly even though they are foreign agents.

Sometimes, women produce *antisperm antibodies*. These antibodies attach to the sperm and prevent them from making their journey to the egg. A man can also produce antibodies to his own sperm. Recurrent miscarriage may also be caused by immunological dysfunction in women.

Infertility-related immune system dysfunction is poorly understood. As a result, only a few tests—and even fewer cures—for this problem exist. Many cases of unexplained infertility are probably caused by unknown immunological problems. Some fertility doctors will treat immune system problems by prescribing drugs to weaken the woman's immune system.

Physical or Mental Stress

Popular belief holds that couples who can't get pregnant just need to relax. This belief fails to recognize that people who are unable to have children feel disappointed, upset, and worried. They may suffer from depression. They may wonder why they aren't like other couples or feel jealous of pregnant women and new babies. Fertility treatment often requires women to take fertility drugs or undergo surgery. Men may feel guilty that their partners—and not themselves—are undergoing painful treatments. Infertile couples find certain holidays—particularly Mother's Day, Father's Day, and Christmas—difficult to face. In short, infertility itself is extremely stressful.

Often, fertility specialists don't try to separate the stress of infertility from other stress but prefer to recommend stress-relief measures overall. These measures may include cutting back on a busy work schedule, meditation, or counseling to reduce marital tension.

Support groups can also be very useful for couples experiencing fertility problems. The national organization, RESOLVE, has many local chapters around the country. Founded by Barbara Eck Menning in 1974, RESOLVE provides cutting-edge information on fertility treatment as well as emotional support. The organization recognizes that infertility has psychological, as well as physical, elements. Menning named her organization RESOLVE because she considered helping people find resolution, through either medical treatment, adoption, or childfree living, as one of the group's most important goals.

The Emotional Impact of Infertility

Infertility is often extremely difficult to bear. People with fertility problems may feel as if they have lost their connection to the future; that somehow they have been skipped in the chain of life. Having children one day is an act many people take for granted. When that picture of the future is threatened, it can be devastating.

Patricia Irwin Johnston, an infertility and adoption educator, has written about infertility as a loss—actually several losses—felt by people who cannot have children easily. This includes a loss of control over future plans and their own bodies. People with fertility problems have lost the chance to conceive a child and to serve as a genetic link to the past and future. They have also lost both the physical and emotional pleasures of pregnancy, childbirth, and breast-feeding. Finally, infertility threatens their opportunity to be a parent.

Infertility is unlike other losses in life. Resolving infertility does not mean eliminating all sadness and grief. Throughout the life cycle, many events will serve as reminders of infertility.

Helen Krouse and her husband, Dave, elected to live childfree after medical treatment failed to prevent recurrent miscarriage and ectopic pregnancy. She is comfortable with their decision, but says she still feels melancholy on occasion.

There are times when I see people with children in strollers and think, "Why me? Why can't I have that?" And I'm sure it will hit me again when I should be a grandma and all my friends are becoming grandmas. It will probably also hit me when my friends are going to their children's high school graduations and weddings and their grandchildren's baptisms. For me, all these things will never be. And some of these events kind of make me sad. It's just now when I cry, it's not as long and it's not as hard.

Many people keep their fertility problems private and share their concerns only with close friends or relatives. Even though infertility is a medical condition, not a sexual inadequacy, people struggling with infertility sometimes feel that it is a taboo subject. They are hesitant to share their burden, even with close friends and family. They may feel too ashamed or embarrassed to share their difficulties, believing that their infertility calls into question their femininity or masculinity. It may raise insecurities about their sexuality and draw unwanted attention—or worse, advice—to their sex life. This is unfortunate, but it demonstrates how entrenched certain infertility myths can be.

Here are some common myths about infertility. They often shape the comments of well-meaning relatives and friends who are trying to offer comfort or advice.

- **Getting pregnant just takes time. Relax! Stop worrying!** By the time many couples share their fertility struggles with other people, they have already been trying for several years. Feeling anxious and worried is a reasonable response to a diagnosis of impaired infertility.

- **Infertile couples have a problem with their sex life.** Infertility is usually a medical condition, not a sexual disorder.

- **Infertility is an embarrassing secret.** This attitude also reflects the belief that infertility is a sexual, rather than a medical, problem.
- **Most women get pregnant easily and immediate-**

ly. **Those that don't will never have children**. This myth reflects the reality of millions of unplanned pregnancies that occur in the United States each year. But fertility is best described as a spectrum, with some couples able to achieve pregnancy more quickly than others. Most couples who seek medical treatment for infertility problems will be able to have children.

■ **You may be better off without children. Children can be so exhausting! And think of it: You're preventing world overpopulation**. Certainly some people decide never to reproduce, for a variety of reasons. But this kind of statement ignores the fact that infertile couples are being denied the opportunity to decide whether to have children or not.

■ **Why go through expensive fertility treatments? Why not just adopt?** Adoption is an answer to the desire to parent, but it is not a cure for infertility. The desire of a couple to have a baby together is normal. For this reason, most couples consider medical treatment before looking into adoption. The adoption process has also changed a great deal in the past few decades. Adoption itself can be expensive, time-consuming, and fraught with uncertainty. The costs of adopting a healthy baby in the United States or from another country can easily exceed $10,000 or even $15,000.[3]

2

DIAGNOSING

FERTILITY

PROBLEMS

The decision to see a doctor for fertility problems can be a very difficult one. One partner, often the woman, may believe there is a problem before the other. If a couple has been trying to have a baby for more than a year, fertility specialists recommend seeking medical advice.

People who mistakenly believe that infertility is the result of a sexual problem may feel ashamed or embarrassed about seeing a doctor. Others may worry that the doctor will immediately try to talk them into expensive treatments. They may be scared by what they have heard about treatment, believing that it is always painful or always produces triplets. Some people will avoid seeking care because they are convinced there is no cure for their problem.

Couples seeking a diagnosis usually begin their quest with their family doctor or the woman's gynecologist, a doctor specializing in the female reproductive tract. Finding the cause of a couple's infertility is not easy. The diagnosis is made after a series of appointments and laboratory tests. The steps the doctor takes to determine a diagnosis is known as an infertility workup. The workup includes recording the medical history of both the man and the woman, conducting a physical exam on both, and scheduling laboratory tests. The workup may take several months, or more, to complete.

During the infertility workup, the doctor is a medical detective. He or she must track down the source of the fertility problem by considering all possible causes. Is the problem with the man's sperm? The woman's fallopian tubes? What about their hormone levels? The doctor knows that the problem may rest with either the man or the woman—or both. For this reason, the doctor will want to schedule examinations and tests for both partners. Testing or treating only one partner is a waste of time. It makes no sense, for example, for a woman to begin taking fertility drugs if her partner's sperm has never been analyzed.

Although a family doctor or gynecologist may begin the infertility workup, physicians specializing in fertility medicine will usually conduct the more advanced tests. Fertility specialists are known as reproductive endocrinologists. The male partner may see an andrologist, a doctor who treats male reproductive disorders.

The infertility workup begins with the physician asking both the man and the woman about their medical history. The doctor will ask questions about their jobs and daily habits to determine if any environmental risks may be affecting fertility. Do they smoke? Drink alcohol? Use street drugs? Next he or she will ask questions about each individual's sexual development since adolescence, the use of birth control, history of sexually transmitted diseases, previous pregnancies, and how often the couple has intercourse. Many people are uncomfortable sharing such intimate details with a doctor and for this reason may resist seeking medical help.

Physical exams are a crucial part of the infertility workup. The woman's physical exam will include an internal pelvic exam to determine whether the size, shape, and position of the woman's cervix, uterus, ovaries, and fallopian tubes are normal. The man's physical exam will include careful examination and *palpation* of the testes, penis, and scrotum. Taking blood to examine hormone levels is an important part of the workup for both men and women. So is testing for the presence of sexually transmitted disease.

The doctor will consider the results of the medical histories and the physical exams and then schedule additional tests. A variety of tests are used during the infertility workup. These tests tend to change, with new tests replacing old, as fertility medicine advances.

Of course, not every couple will have every test. The infertility workup is a flexible process, rather than a series of rigid steps. In a sense, the workup is customized to address each couple's particular situation. For these reasons, the infertility workup varies from couple to couple.

The physician decides which tests are necessary. The discoveries made during one step of the process guide the direction of the doctor's next step. During the medical history, for example, a man will state whether he has fathered children in the past, perhaps in a previous marriage. If he has fathered children, his physician will suspect that it is the woman who has a fertility problem.

When scheduling laboratory tests, the doctor typically begins with the simplest tests—those that require only minor preparation or discomfort. If the simple tests offer no answers, more involved tests—including some that require surgery—may follow. The doctor uses the laboratory tests to determine whether the couple is meeting the four criteria needed for conception to occur:

- Is the woman ovulating properly?

- Is the man producing enough healthy sperm?

- Can the egg and sperm unite in the fallopian tube?

- Can the fertilized egg implant in the uterus?

No single test can answer all four questions, of course. Different tests provide different types of information. For this reason, some couples may undergo many tests before uncovering the cause of their infertility.

Is Ovulation Occurring?

One of the first things the doctor will want to determine is whether the woman is ovulating normally. A woman can do this by taking her *basal body temperature* with an oral thermometer every morning before getting out of bed. When ovulation occurs, the body temperature usually rises 0.5°F (0.3°C). This slight rise is the result of increased production of progesterone. Her temperature will decrease when the woman gets her period, and her menstrual cycle begins again.

By keeping a basal body temperature chart, a woman can determine when she is most fertile. This chart is an important part of the couple's infertility workup. A home kit sold in drugstores, which detects luteinizing hormone in urine, can also be used to test for ovulation.

Sperm Analysis

Although sperm analysis is the most important test conducted on the man, many men are reluctant to have their sperm tested. They may believe their sperm count is a sign of their virility. They also may feel embarrassed about providing the sample. To provide a sperm sample, the man must masturbate into a sterile container while in a private room at the doctor's office. Although this may seem awkward, it is the best way to ensure a fresh, uncontaminated sample.

Immediately after receiving the sperm sample, the man's doctor examines it under a microscope. The doctor will examine the shape of the sperm cells for abnormalities. Studies have shown that 50 percent of the sperm must be well-formed for fertilization to occur. The physician will also examine how well the sperm swim forward and estimate how many sperm cells are present, sometimes with the help of a computer. Ideally, a man will produce at least 20 million sperm per milliliter of semen, although a man with high-quality sperm may still be able to father children despite a low sperm count.

The number of sperm cells in a man's ejaculate can vary from week to week. A single low sperm count may not be typical of a man's overall sperm production. For this reason, the doctor will want to examine at least two or three samples taken over several weeks.

Several tests are available to determine whether the egg and sperm can unite. One test, called the sperm penetration assay, uses a hamster egg to test the sperm's ability to penetrate the egg's outer layer. It is also called the hamster test. No strange human-hamster creatures can result from this test. Although a healthy sperm can penetrate the egg, it cannot fertilize it.

Another test for sperm quality, done several hours after the man and woman have had intercourse, is used to determine whether the man's sperm is able to survive the trip through the cervix. This is known as the *postcoital test* or *Sims-Hühner test*. The woman must make an office visit to her doctor where a sample of her cervical mucus is taken and the sperm found there are studied. The doctor checks for cervical mucus incompatibility by examining the ability of the sperm to swim in the mucus.

This test must be performed just before ovulation, so mistiming the test one month means waiting an entire month to try again. To further complicate matters, many couples find it difficult to have scheduled sex. Having sex as part of a medical workup creates enormous tension and, frequently, arguments. Many couples find it impossible to make love the night before their postcoital test. For this reason, the postcoital test is often canceled and rescheduled.

More invasive tests may be used during the infertility workup to take a closer look at the body. Structural problems in the uterus, fallopian tubes, and pelvis can be diagnosed with a *hysterosalpingogram (HSG)*. This is an X ray of the uterus and fallopian tubes made after dye is injected into the uterus via the cervix. The dye travels through the uterus and tubes. Any obstruction in the reproductive system is marked by where the dye flow stops. One of the most important things the HSG can do is determine whether the fallopian tubes are open.

A small sample of the tissue from the lining of the uterus after ovulation can tell the doctor whether the lining is normal. The lining of the uterus, known as the *endometrium*, should thicken after ovulation to prepare for the implantation of a fertilized egg. This test is known as an *endometrial biopsy*.

Surgery

Surgery may be a part of the workup. Although it can provide important information about structural defects, surgery also poses several risks. Some people don't respond well to anesthesia. Surgery also carries risks of bleeding, swelling, and infection. Very rarely, the surgeon makes a mistake. The decision to undergo surgery should never be made lightly.

Looking inside the body with a special tube, directly at a woman's reproductive organs, is necessary to diagnose endometriosis. It can also determine whether scar tissue covering the ovaries or tubes may be affecting fertility. The procedure, known as *laparoscopy*, is performed in a hospital operating room and the woman must be under general anesthesia. The woman's abdominal cavity is inflated with carbon dioxide so that the doctor has more room to look around.

To look inside, the doctor makes a tiny incision inside the belly button and inserts a thin fiber-optic viewing device with a light on the end. The images are often projected onto a video screen. Another incision may be made below the pubic hairline so that the doctor can insert instruments to

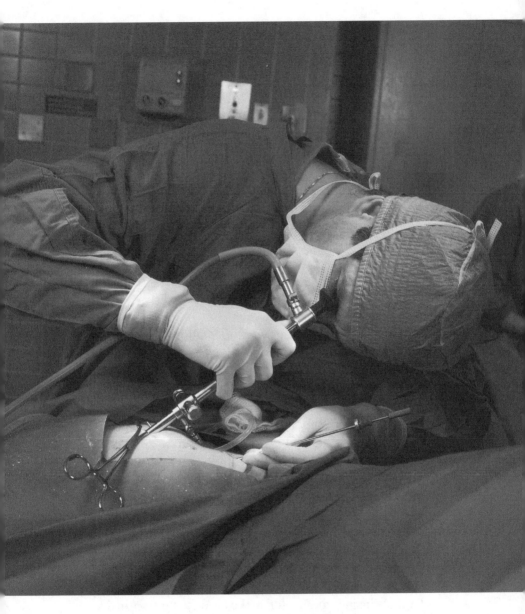

For women with endometriosis or blocked tubes, laparoscopy can be an important part of the fertility workup.

gently lift organs for a better view or remove endometrial scar tissue.

In men, a medical examination of the sperm-producing cells can reveal the reason for a low sperm count. To do this, the doctor must remove a very small tissue sample from inside the testicle. This is known as a *testicular biopsy*. The man may be under general anesthesia in an operating room, or he may have the procedure done with local anesthesia. If the biopsy shows that sperm production is normal, then the physician will suspect that the problem lies with an obstruction somewhere in the sperm ducts.

After the Workup

Ideally, the infertility workup will reveal the problems that are interfering with a couple's ability to conceive. Once a couple has a diagnosis in hand, they will be able to evaluate the medical treatments available to treat their condition. Many of these couples will be helped by fertility drugs, corrective surgery, or other conventional treatments.

Unfortunately, about 20 percent of couples who have a workup will be told that no specific cause for their infertility can be found. They will receive a diagnosis of unexplained infertility instead.

3

CONVENTIONAL

TREATMENTS

Not every couple that undergoes an infertility workup and learns why they are unable to conceive a baby will continue with medical treatment. Howard Jones, a renowned American fertility specialist, estimates that 43 percent of women with fertility problems seek a medical reason for their failure to conceive. Of that group, only 24 percent continue with medical treatment after they have received a diagnosis.[1] In other words, only about 10 percent of all women with fertility problems undergo a fertility workup and then enter treatment. However, many of the women in that small group—estimates range from 50 to 65 percent—will become pregnant.

Jones's data comes from the 1988 National Survey of Family Growth conducted by the National Center for Health Statistics. The survey asked a large sample of women aged 15 to 44 years about their lifetime reproductive history. The survey found that 9.1 percent of the women had impaired fertility. Of that group, only 43 percent sought advice or treatment for their problem. About one-quarter of these women were given advice for pinpointing ovulation, 21 percent underwent diagnostic testing, 20 percent took fertility drugs, 9.8 percent had surgery for blocked tubes, 4.7 percent attempted assisted insemination, and 1.8 percent underwent in vitro fertilization.[2]

The decision to continue with medical treatment is intensely personal. Some people may have deeply held religious or personal beliefs that steer them away from treatment. Others may wish to consider adoption immediately. Still others may decide to live without children. Young couples with only mildly impaired fertility, perhaps due to limited endometriosis or a slightly low sperm count, may be willing to give themselves more time to get pregnant on their own before they seek medical help.

Most couples decide to explore medical treatment before making the decision to adopt. It's very typical, however, for one partner to be more interested in medical treatment and one to be more interested in adoption. John and Lisa Veerlos (not their real names) considered adoption after they learned that John produced few sperm, but chose to undergo medical treatment instead. Lisa says that many people didn't understand their decision.

> *It always seems to be that people's first response is, "Oh, you're going through treatment again? Why don't you just stop and adopt? Why are you doing this to yourself when you could just so easily adopt? My neighbor down the street did."*

John adds:

> *My mind has changed a lot regarding adoption. I used to think that adoption was the solution. But then all these troubling adoption cases started coming up. This thing happened or that thing happened and you see a person who thinks they've reached closure and 6 months later someone comes and takes the child away. I realize it's the rare case that*

this happens. But it gets the publicity and draws awareness to that one negative aspect and it starts nagging in the back of your head.

Couples leaning toward beginning medical treatment will want to carefully consider the cost and effort as well as the likelihood of pregnancy resulting.

Fertility treatment can be very expensive. Although people expect surgery to be costly, they may be unprepared for the outrageous expenses of some fertility drugs. One monthly cycle with the powerful drug Pergonal, for instance, can cost more than $1,000.

Unfortunately, many health insurance companies in the United States refuse to pay to treat infertility. Insurance companies say they are reluctant to cover the costs of treatment because infertility is not a serious health condition and treating it can be very expensive. If they covered infertility, their argument goes, it would add too much to the cost of the health insurance premiums paid by all their customers. But advocates for infertile couples disagree and argue that infertility is a physical disorder that deserves coverage.

Of course, even if infertility treatment were covered by insurance, it wouldn't solve the problem for everyone. Many people in the United States lack health insurance or have limited insurance. Sadly, the high cost of fertility treatment, especially for those without good health insurance, prevents many couples from seeking medical help. These people are shut out of treatment altogether.

What happens to people who cannot decide what to do about their fertility problems? Unable to afford treatment and unwilling to look into adoption, they may continue to hope for a baby even if they know the odds of conceiving are slim.

Year after year, the announcement of a friend's pregnancy or the arrival of Mother's Day is devastating. Concerns about infertility may overshadow the rest of life. Psychologically, people can get stuck feeling very bad about themselves and their lives. RESOLVE was founded in part to help these people. By offering support and education, RESOLVE helps people learn to deal with their fertility problems in new and healthier ways.

Starting Fertility Treatment

Couples who enter infertility treatment face a bewildering assortment of options. Drugs, surgery, and assisted insemination are all considered conventional treatments for infertility. Although they may sound pretty unconventional at times, this label is used to distinguish them from high-tech procedures in which conception occurs outside of the body, as with in vitro fertilization.

Understanding fertility treatment can be confusing because the same approach can be used to address a variety of different problems. For instance, a woman may take fertility drugs because she has a problem with ovulation, a single blocked fallopian tube, or a partner with a low sperm count. Fertility drugs are also prescribed during in vitro fertilization.

There is rarely only one treatment for an infertility problem. Often, several treatments are available. The treatments are often described as ranging from conservative to aggressive, based upon the severity of their side effects. Physicians typically want to try the least aggressive approach first; drugs before surgery, for instance, and conventional treatments before in vitro fertilization. However, couples who feel they are running out of time may want to move quickly toward aggressive solutions if more conservative options fail.

Treating Infertility in Women

Treating Ovulatory Disorders

Hormonal medications, also called fertility drugs, can help a couple overcome problems with ovulation. *Clomiphene*, sold as a pill under the brand name Clomid or Serophene, induces ovulation by stimulating the pituitary gland. The side effects of this pill include nausea and vomiting, mood swings, headaches, and breast tenderness. Clomiphene may also stimulate more than one egg to mature per cycle, thus increasing the chance of having twins to 5 or 10 percent. (Slightly more than 1 percent of births—about 1 in 90— result in twins naturally.) If pregnancy doesn't occur after four to six cycles of clomiphene, stronger drugs may be recommended.

A more powerful (and more expensive) fertility drug is *human menopausal gonadotropin (hMG)*. This medication is sold under the brand names Pergonal and Humegon, and contains follicle-stimulating hormone and luteinizing hormone. For years, the company that sold Pergonal obtained the ingredients for the drug by collecting the urine of Catholic nuns who were past menopause. Pergonal and Humegon are given by injection into the buttocks or upper thigh.

The drug's potential side effects are dangerous enough that a woman on hMG must make frequent, even daily, visits to the fertility clinic. She undergoes *ultrasound* examination and has a blood test to make sure that her ovaries are not in danger of being overstimulated. If they are, her drug dosage is adjusted.

Ovarian *hyperstimulation* occurs when ovaries swell and excess fluid collects in the abdominal cavity. Without proper *monitoring*, a woman's ovaries may burst, causing massive internal hemorrhaging and possibly death.

Another serious side effect of hMG is the heightened risk of multiple fetuses, including the possibility of triplets or more. Multiple fetuses, mostly twins, occur in about 20 percent of the women who use this drug. The hazards of becoming pregnant with multiples is discussed further in Chapter 7.

Treating Abnormal Hormone Levels

Drug therapy is often used for a variety of hormonal disorders, including polycystic ovarian disease and conditions related to the thyroid or pituitary gland. Drugs can be used to correct imbalances of specific hormones. Recurrent miscarriage, in some cases, can be prevented by administering progesterone. Progesterone can be given by injection or as a vaginal suppository.

A woman whose ovaries are completely incapable of producing eggs as a result of premature menopause may still be able to experience pregnancy and birth if she is willing to undergo in vitro fertilization with her partner's sperm and eggs donated by another woman. Although her partner will have a genetic connection to their baby, she will not. Otherwise, adoption is her only option for starting a family. Chapter 6 will look at the medical and ethical use of donor eggs in detail.

Treating Endometriosis

Since the connection between endometriosis and infertility is poorly understood, doctors disagree on the proper treatment of an infertility patient with endometriosis. Some doctors believe that slowing the growth of endometrial tissue with drugs will improve the odds of conception. Other doctors recommend surgery to remove the dense tissue. The problem with this treatment option is that endometriosis often continues, and may even worsen, despite treatment.

If a woman with endometriosis still fails to become pregnant after drug treatment or surgery, her doctor may recommend in vitro fertilization. Some doctors believe IVF is less risky and invasive than repeated surgeries. IVF is not a cure for endometriosis, obviously, but it will surmount the problems with fertilization that are caused by endometriosis. The use of IVF to treat infertility caused by endometriosis is controversial.

Treating Blocked or Missing Fallopian Tubes

Tubal blockages can be removed by cutting them out with a scalpel or burning them away with a laser. In a procedure known as *balloon tuboplasty*, a tiny uninflated balloon is threaded inside the tube and then inflated. If only one tube is obstructed, some doctors will prescribe fertility drugs to boost a woman's chance of conception every other month as she ovulates on the side where the healthy tube is located. This may be more appealing to her than surgery.

If the tubes are blocked beyond surgical repair, then the egg has no chance of ever meeting the sperm. IVF becomes the only option available to a couple who wishes to create a baby from their own egg and sperm. A physician must retrieve the egg from the ovary, place it in a laboratory dish, and add sperm. The fertilized egg is then returned by the physician to the uterus. Chapter 5 will look at IVF in more detail.

Treating Cervical Mucus Incompatibility

Cervical mucus incompatibility can be treated with intrauterine insemination. Some doctors may recommend IVF if pregnancy doesn't occur after several attempts.

Treating Uterine Disorders

Some problems with the shape and structure of the uterus can be solved with surgery. A surgical procedure can be performed to remove an abnormal wall of tissue, known as a *septum*, that sometimes appears in the middle of the uterus. Uterine fibroid tumors can also be removed.

A woman who ovulates normally but whose uterus is incapable of carrying a pregnancy may seek out another woman who is willing to carry an embryo produced with her egg and her partner's sperm. The egg is fertilized in the laboratory, through IVF, and the resulting embryo is transferred into the uterus of the second woman. The use of a *host uterus* is discussed further in Chapter 6. Otherwise, adoption is the only other parenting option available to a woman with severe uterine disorders.

Treating Infertility in Men

Treating Low Sperm Count or Unhealthy Sperm

A man with abnormal sperm or a low sperm count can try to improve the quality of his sperm. By working with his doctor, the man may be able to identify the cause of his infertility and seek treatment. Frequent trips to an overheated atmosphere, like a hot tub or sauna, or the presence of bacterial or viral infection may temporarily lower a man's sperm count. Avoiding heat or treating the infection should raise that man's sperm count.

Unfortunately, in about half of the men with sperm abnormalities, the cause is unknown. This startlingly statistic reveals our ignorance about male infertility. Further research is needed to better understand the factors responsible for healthy sperm production.

It may seem that even a man with a low sperm count or other sperm problems can still expect to achieve pregnancy. After all, it takes only one normal sperm to fertilize an egg. Yet the odds are stacked steeply against such a man fathering a baby. Don't forget that during sexual intercourse, roughly 20 million to 100 million sperm are normally released. That many sperm are needed to ensure that even one survives the difficult journey through the cervix, uterus, and fallopian tubes to fertilize the egg.

At present, no treatments exist that can directly improve the quality of a man's sperm. Fertility drugs will stimulate a woman's ovaries to produce eggs, but no drug exists that can stimulate a man's testes to produce more or better sperm. Instead, medical treatments for poor sperm quality focus on helping the sperm and egg meet. At the same time, the man's partner is often given fertility drugs so that there are more eggs available to the sperm. This strategy boosts the likelihood that even one sperm will fertilize one egg.

Intrauterine insemination is one way to increase the odds that sperm will reach the egg. As you learned earlier, the sperm sample is obtained through masturbation. The sample is processed by a technician to separate the sperm from the semen fluids. Semen fluids, in some men, may actually play a role in preventing fertilization. Sperm washing will also remove any harmful bacteria from the sample. The physician uses a sterile plastic syringe or thin tube to place the sperm inside the woman's uterus. This is a relatively simple and painless procedure that takes place in the doctor's office and lasts just a few minutes. This procedure gives the sperm a "free ride" through the cervix, allowing more sperm than normal to reach the uterus and, hopefully, the tubes.

Some doctors recommend in vitro fertilization for men with low sperm counts or abnormal sperm, although its use for this purpose is controversial. Those physicians who support it argue that this is another way of helping the sperm reach the egg. IVF goes one step further than intrauterine insemination. With IVF, the sperm is actually placed right next to several eggs in a laboratory dish. Compared to natural fertilization, fewer sperm—150,000 rather than 20 million to 100 million—are needed for laboratory fertilization.

The ultimate method of uniting sperm and egg involves actually injecting a single sperm into the egg itself. The technique, known as *intracytoplasmic sperm injection (ICSI)*, is especially useful for sperm that lack movement or the ability to penetrate an egg. ICSI is an extra step that can be added to an IVF cycle to ensure that fertilization occurs. This new procedure is discussed in more detail in Chapter 5.

At present, men who produce no sperm at all have no medical treatment available to them. If the couple wants to experience pregnancy and birth together, their only option is donor sperm. It can be a shock to receive this diagnosis. Paul White describes how he and his wife, Carole, felt when they sought an answer for their fertility problems.

I had zero sperm. There were no sperm there to extract out. ICSI was not an option. It was very tough. Carole and I both cried when the doctor first told us about it. It's not something you even think about. You always feel, from the time you're very young, that you're going to have the opportunity to procreate and have children.

I am my father's only son, so his lineage basically ends as far as me producing an heir from his lineage is concerned. You find yourself thinking in those terms whether or not you believe them to be important. I think the first thing I thought through was the impact of the diagnosis on Carole and my parents. It took me a little while to think about the actual loss that I faced. I would never father a child. I could be a father to a child, but I would never father a child.

After receiving the doctor's diagnosis, Paul and Carole decided to use *donor sperm* to build their family.

Donor sperm comes from a man other than the woman's husband or partner. It is collected from men who remain anonymous to the infertile couple and is available through a sperm bank, a medical facility set up for this purpose. Intrauterine insemination is used to place the sperm in the woman's body. Sometimes the doctor places the sperm in the vagina or the cervix instead of the uterus.

With donor sperm, only the woman has a genetic link to the baby. Couples faced with male infertility may also look into adoption to build their family.

Treating Varicocele

If a varicocele, or varicose vein, is present on the scrotum, surgery can correct the problem. In some men, removing the varicocele leads to an improvement in semen quality. Surgery can also be used to clear an obstruction in the sperm ducts or to reverse a vasectomy.

Treating Other Causes of Infertility

Treating Immune System Dysfunction

Fertility specialists do not agree on how to treat immune system dysfunctions. Some physicians believe that the chance of conception can be improved by deliberately weakening the woman's immune system with steroid drugs. This way, the theory goes, the woman's body won't attack the sperm or embryo as a foreign agent. Unfortunately, weakening the immune system can cause serious side effects and leave the woman vulnerable to infection. The usefulness of such an approach still needs to be demonstrated with a large scientific study.

Treating Unexplained Infertility

Unexplained infertility is an extremely disheartening diagnosis. It's also discouragingly common. About 20 percent of couples who undergo a fertility workup are told that no physical cause for their infertility can be identified. The frequency of this diagnosis illustrates how much is still unknown about human reproduction and infertility.

To treat unexplained infertility, the doctor may urge the couple to simply keep trying. He or she may suggest that they boost their chances of conception by avoiding caffeine, alcohol, and drugs, and by charting ovulation. If the couple wants to pursue a more aggressive approach, perhaps because of the woman's age, the doctor may prescribe fertility drugs. If that fails, the couple may then ask to try a more powerful fertility drug. Or they may want to try several cycles of drugs combined with intrauterine insemination. If pregnancy still doesn't occur, the couple and their doctor may consider IVF, although the use of in vitro fertilization for unexplained infertility is controversial.

Coping With Treatment

For the couples who are going through the series of doctor visits and medical techniques that make up infertility treatment, it is an all-encompassing process that touches every aspect of their lives. Here is how actress JoBeth Williams described treatment for herself and her husband when she spoke in 1989 before a congressional subcommittee that was investigating fertility clinics.

We didn't know why we weren't getting pregnant and everybody just seemed to tell us, relax and don't think about it, which isn't possible because, at that point, I would cry every time I saw a mother and a baby. This was about the sixth year of trying, I guess. I felt angry and jealous every time I saw a pregnant woman. When several of my friends became pregnant, I couldn't be around them because I found it too painful.

I had a tremendous sense of failure. It was so strong that I began to feel that I must be guilty of something but I didn't know of what. I felt like I was being punished. I felt like the fact that I couldn't do the very thing that my body was designed to do, to conceive and carry a child, must mean that I wasn't fully a woman in some way. All my other accomplishments in life seemed to fade into the background in the face of this failure.[3]

Emotionally, infertility treatment is a roller coaster of highs and lows. Each monthly cycle begins with new hope and then, all too often, ends in crushing disappointment and grief. Until the couple finds some resolution to their fertility problems, this cycle will repeat itself over and over.

Infertility treatment also threatens to overwhelm daily life. Frequent doctor visits to monitor the use of fertility drugs disrupt work routines and may prevent overnight travel for business or pleasure. The drugs themselves cause mood swings, bloating, and depression, and injection sites may be sore. Financially, the couple may be struggling to save money for treatment or fighting to get their health insurer to cover more of the costs. Making love according to the calendar or a doctor's orders can cause anxiety and stress and may lead to sexual difficulties.

If the couple hasn't told friends or family about their fertility problems, they may find it stressful to conceal the purpose of doctor visits. The secrecy may add to their feelings of isolation or depression. On the other hand, people who tell others about their fertility treatment open themselves up to nosy questions and unwanted advice.

Many fertility clinics recommend that couples seek out counseling or a support group like RESOLVE during this period. Taking care of themselves emotionally is as important as taking care of themselves physically. If one medical treatment fails, counseling can help couples decide on their next step, whether it be adoption, living without children, or more aggressive treatment.

Only a very few couples, less than 5 percent of those in medical treatment, will go on to use high-tech procedures in which conception occurs outside of the body. Although high-tech procedures are rarely necessary to successfully treat infertility, their existence represents an enormous medical accomplishment. At the same time, assisted reproduction raises significant ethical concerns. For these reasons, many pages in this book have been devoted to a discussion of in vitro fertilization and other high-tech procedures.

4

THE

FIRST

IN VITRO

BABY

On July 25, 1978, Louise Brown was born in England. The world greeted the news of her birth with excitement and awe. Louise Brown was no ordinary baby; she represented a stunning medical achievement. She was the first baby ever born who was conceived outside her mother's body. One British newspaper called her "Our Miracle Baby." Another dubbed Louise, "Baby of the Century." Most every other news source jubilantly referred to Louise as a "test-tube baby."[1]

The term "test-tube baby" is still used to describe the more than 30,000 babies who have been conceived in laboratories all over the world since 1978. As you know, bringing together eggs and sperm in the laboratory is called in vitro fertilization. (*In vitro* is Latin, meaning "in glass." In the modern lab, however, glass has given way to plastic.) Both of the terms used for this high-tech method of fertilization emphasize that the egg and sperm are united, not in a fallopian tube, but in a plastic laboratory dish.

On July 25, 1978, Louise Brown became the world's first "test tube baby." Here, 15-month-old Louise is shown with her parents, Lesley and John.

In vitro fertilization consists of a series of steps that must be carefully timed. First, one or more mature eggs are surgically removed from the woman's ovary. The eggs are placed in a flat-bottomed laboratory dish with sperm. If one of the sperm fertilizes the egg, the egg is allowed to grow for 2 or 3 days in the lab. During that time, it will divide several times until it is a cluster of four or eight cells. In the final step, the fertilized egg is placed in the mother's uterus with a plastic tube inserted through the vagina and cervix. There it remains for a normal pregnancy and birth.

Louise Brown's birth marked a new era in medicine and morality. Would this procedure allow rich women to hire poor women to carry their babies? Could it be used to select embryos with certain characteristics? What if embryos belonging to two different couples were accidentally—or intentionally—swapped? Was it ethical to destroy a fertilized egg in the laboratory? These pressing questions, which accompanied the arrival of baby Louise, are with us still.

Yet despite such serious social and ethical concerns, the world's response to Louise was overwhelmingly positive. It's easy to see why. The men responsible for the medical achievement, gynecologist Patrick C. Steptoe and physiologist Robert G. Edwards, spoke only of their desire to help infertile couples. Louise's parents, Lesley and John, unable to have a baby together for many years, looked the picture of happiness holding their new daughter. And the end result of this scientific experiment was no complicated piece of technology or difficult-to-understand concept but rather a beautiful baby girl. No wonder the world rejoiced along with the Browns.

In vitro fertilization is the cornerstone of assisted reproductive technology. It is the procedure that has led to many sensationalistic headlines in recent years. With IVF, a woman can become pregnant with her own egg or the egg of another woman. She may use IVF to become pregnant with her husband's sperm or the sperm of an anonymous donor.

With IVF, a woman can give her egg, fertilized by the sperm of her husband, to another woman who has agreed to carry the pregnancy to term and to relinquish the newborn baby to its genetic parents. Before the success of Steptoe and Edwards, these fantastic scenarios were the stuff of science fiction. With the birth of Louise Brown, the fiction was transformed into reality.

The Scientists: Patrick C. Steptoe and Robert G. Edwards

Patrick C. Steptoe began his career as an obstetrician and gynecologist after serving as a physician in World War II. He worked at Oldham General and District Hospital in Oldham, a town near Manchester in northwest England. In the late 1950s and early 1960s, Steptoe invented the laparoscope, a 12-inch (30-cm)-long tube with an eyepiece and its own light that allowed a physician to look directly at the interior of the abdomen without performing a major operation. Of course, the laparoscope that Steptoe built looks extremely primitive compared to the sophisticated device used today. Damaged or missing fallopian tubes were among the conditions Steptoe could see when he examined a woman with his laparoscope.

Steptoe described using the laparoscope to perform surgery in a medical paper that was published in 1965. One of the medical scientists who read that paper was Robert G. Edwards, a physiologist at Cambridge University. Edwards had perfected a technique for fertilizing human eggs in the laboratory. The eggs Edwards used came from women whose ovaries had been surgically removed.

Edwards contacted Steptoe and the two began to collaborate in 1966. By combining their expertise, they hoped one day to be able to remove an egg from a healthy woman, fertilize it in the laboratory, and then place it in the uterus. If successful, their efforts would enable women with hopelessly blocked fallopian tubes to become pregnant.

Steptoe began to investigate the use of fertility drugs for stimulating maturation of the eggs in the ovary. Edwards invented a device that could be used to collect mature eggs from the ovaries. By 1971, they were confident of their ability to retrieve an egg and fertilize it in the lab. Now they were ready to place the fertilized egg in a woman's uterus. In 4 years they made more than sixty attempts to achieve a pregnancy. Their volunteers were women with damaged fallopian tubes who were so eager to become pregnant that they were willing to undergo the scientists' unproven, experimental procedure. In 1975, Steptoe and Edwards finally had a success but then discovered that the embryo implanted in the wrong place—a deformed fallopian tube rather than the uterus. The ectopic pregnancy was ended after 13 weeks.

During the time of their early experiments, Steptoe and Edwards faced hostile criticism from many people, including members of Parliament, conservative clergymen, and fellow scientists. They were accused of risking the birth of babies with defects. To some, the implications of their research were ominous and the team was accused of playing God. The British Medical Research Council declared that more research on primates was needed and refused to fund the scientists' work.

As a result of these attacks, Steptoe and Edwards were very reluctant to discuss their experiments publicly or to publish their findings in medical journals. Using money Steptoe earned by performing legal abortions, the men continued their experiments with volunteer patients who hoped this experimental infertility treatment would make them pregnant.

The Parents: Lesley Brown and Gilbert John Brown

In 1977, at the age of 29, Lesley Brown was ready to seek medical help for her infertility. In the factory where she wrapped cheese for supermarkets, she had seen most of the other women become mothers. She envied their pregnancies and the babies they brought in for their friends to see. Year after year she waited for her baby to come. Her husband, John, a truck driver, had children from a previous marriage, but after almost a decade of marriage they had none together. In 1970, she had been told that she had blocked fallopian tubes, but she hoped that future medical advances might be able to help her.

At her local medical clinic, Lesley learned about Steptoe's research. Desperate, she and John made an appointment with Steptoe and traveled 4 hours by train from their home in Bristol to Oldham. As they had little money, taking time off from work and making this trip strained their finances. When John won £800 (about $1,500) betting in a soccer pool, he decided it was a good omen and dedicated it to Steptoe's treatment.

Steptoe described his experimental treatment to Lesley. He cautioned that it was experimental, but she dismissed his words. "Crazy as it sounds, even when Mr. Steptoe, the gynaecologist, warned me that a baby had never been successfully conceived outside the womb, I still wouldn't believe him," she declared later in *Our Miracle Named Louise*, the book she and John wrote after the birth.[2] Like many women before and after her, Lesley was willing to take part in a grand medical experiment if it offered the possibility of pregnancy.

On November 10, 1977, at a small institution called Dr. Kershaw's Cottage Hospital, Steptoe removed a mature egg from Lesley's ovary. Today, women undergoing in vitro fertilization are put on a strict regimen of fertility drugs to control and encourage the maturation of eggs. But Lesley was not. To achieve Louise's birth, Steptoe carefully timed his egg retrieval proceedure with Louise's natural menstrual cycle so that he could remove the one mature egg she produced that month.

Lesley's egg was placed in a laboratory petri dish where it was combined with sperm from John. Two-and-a-half days later, Steptoe placed the eight-cell embryo in Lesley's uterus. Lesley spent the next 2 weeks at the Oldham hospital, most of it in bed out of fear of miscarrying. Finally, Lesley returned home to Bristol and by late December her pregnancy was confirmed.

One of the biggest unknowns that faced scientists experimenting with human eggs in the lab was whether the fetus would develop into a healthy baby. Steptoe used ultrasound to make sure Lesley's baby was developing properly. He also removed a small amount of *amniotic fluid* and examined the fetal cells in it for any chromosomal defects. This procedure is known as *amniocentesis*.

If Steptoe had found a deformity in the young fetus, he would have aborted it immediately. Lesley and John had been obligated to agree to this condition before beginning treatment.

News of the anticipated birth began leaking out midway through Lesley's pregnancy. The first news story appeared in the April 19, 1978 edition of the New York *Post*. As public interest mounted, Steptoe went to extraordinary efforts to protect Lesley from the press and to keep the progress of the pregnancy a secret. In June, he persuaded Lesley to enter the Oldham Hospital under the name Rita Ferguson.

Lesley was carefully guarded and did not even venture outside. Similarly, John Brown worked to keep his identity unknown, an increasingly difficult task as he made frequent trips from Bristol to visit Lesley. Finally, in an effort to end their hide-and-seek game with the press, the Browns made a deal for £300,000 (about $565,000) with London's *Daily Mail* for their exclusive story.

Although the Lesley's baby was expected to arrive in early August, Steptoe decided to deliver the baby by *cesarean section* on the evening of July 25. He claimed that Lesley had developed slight signs of *toxemia*, a rare but serious disease of pregnancy that can lead to stillbirth. Like everything else about the pregnancy, the operation was carried out by Steptoe under great secrecy. Even John didn't know the baby was to be born until minutes before Lesley was put under general anesthesia and rolled into the delivery room. The operation, which was filmed by the information agency of the British government, went well, and Louise Joy Brown was delivered 13 minutes before midnight. The 5-pound 12-ounce (2.6-kg) infant was in perfect health.

On July 26, Steptoe and Edwards broke their silence and held a press conference. Lesley, John, and Louise posed for photographers. Pictures from that press conference show Steptoe and Edwards looking both elated and relieved. "The last time I saw her, she was a beautiful eight-celled embryo," Edwards gushed.[3]

New Technology Brings New Questions

Not all the voices that heralded Louise's birth found it so praiseworthy. The day after Louise was born, Roman Catholic leaders criticized IVF as they had criticized intrauterine insemination in the past. Statements from the pope have consistently condemned any form of reproduction that separates procreation from sexual intercourse in marriage.

Although other religions have been more open to assisted reproduction than the Catholic Church, the use of donor sperm or eggs is forbidden by several faiths. According to Judaism, *gamete* donation breaks the genetic connection between generations and muddies issues of lineage, legitimacy, and genealogy. Islamic law considers the use of donor sperm to be a form of adultery.

Fundamental Christianity, Orthodox Judaism, and the Mormon faith are among the religions that place great emphasis on procreation and large families. These religions teach that motherhood is a woman's most important role and that large families deserve to be praised. In such communities, the couple who has decided not to go public with their fertility problems may find themselves the focus of intrusive questioning or, even worse, criticism. The constant focus on creating a family can become very difficult for them to bear. Faced with this difficult situation, some infertile women have found comfort in reading about Hannah, Sarah, Elizabeth, and other Biblical heroines who were unable to bear children.

Assisted reproduction has also drawn attention and criticism from feminist thinkers. This is not surprising, since most of the medical risks related to treatment affect women more than men. In addition, the industry itself is dedicated to motherhood, a role that was once a woman's only option.

The question of why women are willing to submit to the risks of assisted reproduction lies at the heart of feminist concern. What does this say about how women view themselves with—and without—a baby? In a separate, but related question, theorists wonder to what extent the assisted reproductive technologies themselves shape a woman's desire to have a baby, especially a baby born from her own egg. At its most extreme, this line of thinking argues that a woman can have no free choice because choice is conditioned by cultural values.

Other feminists support assisted reproduction for the same reason they support abortion rights—it expands a woman's reproductive choices. These thinkers believe that a woman should have the right to choose IVF and other technologies. Women should not be shielded from the risks of these procedures, but should be allowed to give their free consent once the risks are carefully explained.

Most fertility programs accept only married women. Feminists have argued that it should not be up to the physicians to decide who will benefit from this technology and who will not. They state that single women and lesbians should not be automatically barred from entering a fertility program. Similarly, access to assisted reproductive techniques should be open to all persons, regardless of race, class, or ability to pay, they argue.

At the heart of many critics' comments, including feminist critics, is the issue of informed consent. They argue that until all the potential effects of assisted reproduction are known—including the long-term physical and psychological health of the children born from the procedure—the consent a woman gives for IVF cannot really be said to be informed.

In her book, Lesley Brown expresses gratitude to Steptoe and Edwards for the birth of Louise and plays down the lack of information given to her about in vitro fertilization. She writes, "I don't remember Mr. Steptoe saying his method of producing babies had ever worked, and I certainly didn't ask. I just imagined that hundreds of children had already been born through being conceived outside their mothers' wombs. Having a baby was all that mattered."[4] To so many couples who seek medical help for their empty cradle, having a baby is all that matters. But should it be?

Assisted Reproduction Moves Ahead

Despite the early controversy surrounding Louise Brown's birth, the world's next IVF births—in Scotland, England, and Australia—followed quickly.

On December 28, 1981, Elizabeth Carr became the first baby fertilized in a laboratory to be born in the United States. She was conceived with help from Howard and Georgeanna Jones, a husband-and-wife team at Eastern Virginia Medical School in Norfolk, Virginia. Howard Jones was an obstetrician and Georgeanna Jones was an endocrinologist. Several years later, these pioneering physicians established the Jones Institute for Reproductive Medicine, the first fertility clinic in the United States.

In vitro fertilization, which U.S. citizens had viewed with both alarm and amazement from afar, was now taking place in their own country. In June 1982, *Glamour* magazine devoted its monthly survey to the topic of IVF. Of the young female readers who responded, 79 percent believed that IVF was ethical. Among those who thought IVF was unethical, there was little agreement about why not, although one-third indicated that they believed babies should be conceived in an act of love.[5]

One of the most immediate concerns regarding IVF before Louise was born was the health of the infants. To a great extent, these worries were unfounded. Louise Brown was healthy and normal, as were the vast majority of in vitro babies born after her. Birth defects among IVF babies are no more and no less common than among the general population of newborns.

Yet, for reasons that are still unclear, in vitro babies, as a group, tend to be born a bit prematurely. As a result, they tend to weigh less than other babies. This is especially true when multiple births are taken into account, but it's also true of IVF babies born as *singletons*. The mothers of IVF babies are also more likely to be hospitalized during pregnancy and to deliver their babies by cesarean section. By 1 or 2 years of age, however, IVF babies are indistinguishable from the general population of children.[6]

Until the current generation of IVF babies—led by Louise—grows up, the world won't know for sure whether laboratory conception has any effect on their growth, behavior, or ability to produce children. For some observers, this is a critical question. They believe that until all the long-term effects of IVF are known, including the future health of the children, the men and women undergoing IVF treatment cannot be considered fully informed when they give their consent. However IVF has gained widespread acceptance, probably because the immediate result—a healthy baby—seems worth almost any risk.

Although in vitro parents have had difficulties conceiving, they often take to parenthood more easily than most adults. Raising children conceived through IVF seems to be no more challenging—and may actually be less stressful—than raising children conceived naturally.

The quality of parenting in families with in vitro children is superior to that of other families, according to several studies.[7] Mothers of in vitro kids scored higher than mothers of children conceived naturally in warmth, emotional involvement, and interaction with their child. IVF fathers also scored significantly higher on father-child interaction. In relation to the general population, families with IVF children reported less stress and generally felt more positive about their children. IVF parents also stated that they are more overprotective than parents of naturally conceived children.

Clearly, in vitro children are very much wanted children. Their parents are generally older. They're less likely to have siblings, especially siblings close in age. All of these qualities probably influence the positive family relationships observed by social scientists.

Should children conceived in the lab be told about their high-tech beginnings? Some parents, proud of their efforts, say yes. If they saved the lab dish where egg met sperm, they may share it with their child. Other parents say no. They feel like it's none of the child's business. After all, how many parents with kids conceived naturally tell their kids all about the circumstances of their conception? Or they may worry that the child will feel different or be teased if he or she reveals in vitro origins.

Celebrity, rather than teasing, seems to be the only challenge Louise Brown has faced in the years since her birth. Her life, and that of her sister, Natalie, born in 1982 by IVF, has been relatively normal. An article that appeared in *The*

New York Times in 1993, when Louise was 15 years old, was titled, "Celebrated Birth Aside, Teen-Ager Is Typical Now." Lesley and John Brown said they had tried to shield Louise from the press and keep her life as ordinary as possible. According to them, she liked "loud music and stupid clothes" and preferred the companionship of her friends to her parents' company.[8]

5

HIGH-TECH

REPRODUCTION:

A CLOSER

LOOK

The last-ditch hope when conventional treatments fail is in vitro fertilization and other forms of high-tech assisted reproduction. Yet this is another fork in the road for many infertile couples. People who were willing to try conventional treatments may be unwilling to try IVF. For one thing, IVF is extremely expensive.

Cost remains one of the most significant obstacles concerning the use of IVF. Most insurance companies won't cover the cost of IVF, and most Americans cannot afford to pay for it themselves. Activists have changed the laws in ten states—Arkansas, California, Connecticut, Hawaii, Illinois, Maryland, Massachusetts, New York, Rhode Island, and Texas—so that insurers are required to cover IVF, but that still leaves forty states without mandated coverage. In some other countries, like England and Australia, infertility treatment is covered by the national health plan.

The effect of insurance coverage—or the lack thereof—on the rate of IVF procedures is startling. People in Massachusetts, for instance, attempt IVF at five times the national average. This isn't because people in Massachusetts are more likely to have fertility problems, but because Massachusetts is one of the states that requires coverage. Similarly, French couples are five times more likely than American couples to undergo IVF, again because IVF is covered by insurance in France.[1]

Activists argue that the insurance companies that don't cover IVF are short sighted. Couples without insurance coverage for infertility are probably going to try other medical solutions instead, even if they're less effective. Women with blocked tubes, for example, may undergo surgery because they know their insurance will pay for it, even though IVF is less expensive and more effective. In the long run, the consumer activists argue, insurance companies could save money by covering IVF.

Cost is not the only reason people think long and hard before undergoing IVF. They know that the procedure fails far more often than it succeeds. It also raises enormous ethical issues. This has been the case with assisted reproduction ever since Louise Brown was born.

Although IVF is now practiced in countries all over the world, it is still a unique and intensely emotional experience for couples going through treatment. If more eggs are fertilized than can be transferred to the uterus, the couple must face difficult ethical questions concerning the fate of those fertilized eggs. For the woman, IVF is, at times, uncomfortable and even painful.

Emotionally, an IVF cycle may threaten to eclipse every other aspect of the couple's life as they wait to see whether this is the month they achieve pregnancy. The couple knows that each phase of the process is one step closer to success—or failure. They can't help but ask questions like: Were the ovaries stimulated? Were enough eggs retrieved? Did the eggs fertilize? Each step forward is cause for celebration until, after embryo transfer, they wait for an answer to the most important question of all: Has pregnancy begun?

Steptoe and Edwards introduced IVF as a treatment for women whose fallopian tubes were missing or completely blocked by scar tissue from pelvic inflammatory disease or severe endometriosis. Since then, IVF treatment has been offered for other types of infertility, including partially blocked tubes, mild endometriosis, and cervical mucus incompatibility. It has also been used by couples in which the male partner has a low sperm count or other sperm abnormalities. Some fertility programs also use IVF to treat couples with unexplained infertility. Since IVF gives these couples a chance to learn whether their eggs and sperm are capable of combining to create embryos, IVF often pinpoints the cause of their infertility.

Experts agree that IVF is a proven treatment for completely blocked tubes. But they disagree about whether any other infertility problem actually benefits from IVF as compared to conventional infertility treatment, or even no medical treatment at all. An influential 1993 report entitled *Proceed With Care* and written by the Canadian Royal Commission on New Reproductive Technologies, recommended that IVF be offered as treatment only to women with completely blocked tubes.

It stated that using IVF to treat any other infertility diagnoses—including mild endometriosis, partially blocked tubes, or sperm problems—should only be done as part of a research study and that, in such cases, the procedure should be described as an experimental treatment.[2] At the time the report was written, no carefully designed scientific studies had been done to determine the usefulness of IVF for these other conditions.

IVF: How It Works

In vitro fertilization is a four-stage process that spans the length of a woman's menstrual cycle. The IVF process begins with the administration of fertility drugs and ends with *embryo transfer.* After the transfer, the woman and her partner wait to see whether the embryo has implanted. As with natural conception, it is not possible to know for sure whether a woman is pregnant until several weeks after ovulation and fertilization. An IVF cycle, therefore, lasts about 1 month.

Although every fertility clinic follows the same basic steps for IVF, each has its own recipe for success, including the mix of drugs it prescribes, the timetable it follows, and the growth medium it places the embryos in. Other variations in the IVF process can occur during *egg retrieval* and embryo transfer as different clinics follow slightly different procedures. The woman's age and previous physical reactions to fertility treatment are also considered when her doctor designs a treatment plan.

Several important features distinguish the way in vitro fertilization is performed today from the way Steptoe and Edwards first used it. One is the routine use of fertility drugs. These drugs stimulate the women's ovaries to produce five to twelve eggs. If several eggs fertilize successfully, three or more embryos are transferred to the uterus. All this is done in the hope that one embryo will implant and grow into a baby.

This approach makes sense. Think about it. Your odds of hitting a home run in one particular softball game increase the more times you're up at bat. The more shots you take during a basketball game, the better your chance of sinking the ball. If you have a friend who is out of the house often, one phone call is unlikely to find her at home. But if you phone many times in one day, you'll eventually reach her. This method could be called, "Try something enough times and eventually you'll succeed."

Unfortunately, there are enormous pitfalls to this approach when it is applied to IVF. Increasing the numbers of eggs stimulated, eggs retrieved, and embryos transferred does indeed increase the chances of a baby being born. But it also creates two new problems. One is that fertility drugs have many immediate serious, even life-threatening, side effects. There is also concern that fertility drugs may cause ovarian and breast cancer. A 1994 study in the *New England Journal of Medicine* showed an increase in ovarian cancer among women who had used clomiphene for more than 1 year.[3] The shorter the period of time that a woman is on fertility drugs, the better.

The other problem is that transferring multiple embryos increases the likelihood of not just one, but many births: twins, triplets, quadruplets, quintuplets, or more, depending upon how many embryos have been placed in the womb. This may sound like a bonanza for a previously infertile couple, but in reality multiple fetuses spawn a multitude of problems during pregnancy, birth, and beyond. This problem, and the imperfect cures it has spawned, are the subject of Chapter 7.

Stage One: Ovarian Stimulation

In the first stage of IVF, the woman takes fertility drugs to stimulate her ovaries to produce multiple eggs. Although some women receive their injections at the clinic, many husbands learn to give their wives the daily injections. Some women may even learn to inject themselves.

As every teenager knows, hormones are powerful stuff. Some of the same hormones responsible for fertility also signal the start of womanhood in adolescent girls. In teenage boys, testosterone and other hormones trigger puberty. Not only are hormones responsible for physical changes, but they can play havoc with the emotions as well. If, in the very same day, you feel great one moment and horrible the next, hormones may be responsible.

Women on fertility drugs often feel similarly out of control. Their moods may swing wildly from elation to depression. The drugs may also cause their bodies to gain weight and their breasts to swell. Their enlarged ovaries, inside their abdomens, may feel tender and easily jarred. On rare occasions, the ovaries are stimulated too much and grow dangerously large.

The risk of overstimulation is one reason the woman's ovaries must be carefully monitored while she is taking these drugs. Several times a week, or even daily, she returns to the fertility clinic so that her ovaries can be viewed with ultrasound. The clinic also takes daily blood samples to measure her *estradiol* levels to determine how quickly the woman's eggs are maturing.

The other reason the woman's ovaries are watched so carefully is so that another drug—one that induces ovulation—can be given at precisely the right stage in follicular development. Give it too early and the eggs won't be mature in time for egg retrieval. Give it too late and the eggs may ovulate naturally into the fallopian tubes. This drug, known by the brand name Profasi, contains *human chorionic gonadotropin*. It prepares the mature eggs for release from the follicle. Egg retrieval is scheduled 36 hours after Profasi is administered.

Stage Two: Egg Retrieval

Not every woman in treatment proceeds to this stage. According to statistics published in 1996, in vitro fertilization in the United States and Canada has an overall success rate of 18.2 deliveries per initiated cycle. This means only about 19 women out of every 100 who enter treatment will deliver a baby. The other 81 women face disappointment: some very early in the cycle and others weeks later when they miscarry an established pregnancy.

Treatment fails in some couples at the very beginning of the cycle. Indeed, only 87 out of every 100 women who respond to fertility drugs will proceed to the next stage of IVF: egg retrieval. Fertility clinics generally expect ovarian stimulation to result in the production of five to twelve mature eggs. If the woman's body produces too few ripe eggs, the clinic will cancel the scheduled egg retrieval and this IVF cycle will be abandoned.

If, however, several mature eggs are ready and waiting, the couple and their clinic will prepare for egg retrieval.

About 2 hours before the eggs are removed from the woman's ovaries, her partner provides the clinic with a sperm sample obtained through masturbation. His sperm is then washed so that the sperm cells have the best chance to achieve fertilization. If the sample contains too few healthy sperm for fertilization, egg retrieval will be canceled.

Egg retrieval is the step in the IVF process that requires the most skill. It takes place in the clinic and lasts about 30 minutes. The woman lies on her back, as if preparing for a routine gynecological exam. To stay relaxed, she may request a light sedative. To remove the eggs, the fertility specialist inserts a thin, hollow needle in the vagina, through the vaginal wall, and into the ovary. A local anesthetic prevents the woman from feeling any pain in her pelvic region. Ultrasound is used to guide the position of the needle and to identify the follicles with mature eggs.

The eggs are then sucked out of the follicles and placed in a sterile container. Once the physician has completed the procedure, the eggs are carefully examined to make sure they are healthy and mature. Only the best eggs will be mixed with sperm.

Egg retrieval, although still awkward and uncomfortable, is less invasive than it was just a few years ago. It is also less expensive than it used to be, although it continues to be one of the most expensive parts of the process. (The fertility drugs are the other major expense.) In 1992, the average cost of IVF was about $8,000.

At that time, eggs were removed during minor surgery. General anesthesia rendered the woman completely unconscious. The IVF surgeon made a small incision in the abdomen and used a laparoscope to look at the ovaries and fallopian tubes while removing the eggs with a special aspiration system.

Although some fertility clinics still use this method, most use the more recently developed technique described above. The average cost of egg retrieval using the newer method is $6,000 or $7,000.

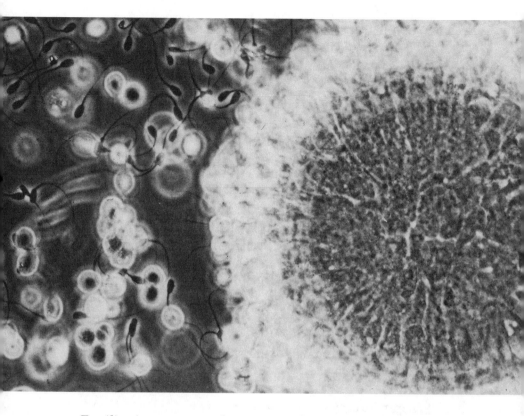

Fertilization occurs at the moment when one sperm cell penetrates an egg cell and their nuclear materials unite. Within hours, the new cell begins to grow and divide as it moves through the fallopian tube toward the uterus.

Stage Three: Fertilization

As soon as the eggs are ready, they are placed with the sperm in a flat-bottomed lab dish. The eggs, too small to be seen with the naked eye, look like translucent blobs under a powerful microscope. The sperm are equally unassuming. Millions of them of them fit easily into a drop or two. But together the egg and sperm have the potential to create a new human life. Those who have seen human conception occur in the lab often describe it in awed terms. Some embryologists—scientists who study fertilization—who have worked with human conception find it incredibly nerve-wracking. They return to animal research and sleep better at night.

The eggs and sperm are incubated at body temperature for 2 or 3 days. If an egg has been fertilized by a sperm, it will begin to divide and grow. This is the earliest stage of embryo development. After 48 hours, the fertilized embryo will consist of four to eight cells. Ideally, three or four eggs will fertilize. If one or more look healthy, the couple and their health care team will prepare for embryo transfer.

In vitro fertilization is best known for this step. Yet, in many ways, this is the easiest and most reliable step. Remember those 87 women who continued on to egg retrieval? Seventy-eight of them will learn that their eggs successfully fertilized in the lab. (Or you could say 90 percent, on average, of those couples who undergo egg retrieval will achieve fertilization.) The couples whose eggs don't fertilize will not go on to embryo transfer. Their IVF cycle will stop here.

Stage Four: Embryo Transfer

Embryo transfer is not a complicated or particularly uncomfortable procedure. No anesthesia is necessary, although some women choose to take a tranquilizer such as Valium. Three or four embryos are placed in a thin plastic tube called a catheter. The catheter is gently inserted through the vagina and into the uterus and the embryos are released. In some clinics, the woman is asked to get on her hands and knees and then raise her hips higher than her head (knee-to-chest position). In other places, the woman lies on her back.

Many clinics permit and even encourage the woman's husband to attend the transfer. Not only does it help the woman relax, but it allows the couple to be together during the creation of their baby—just as they would be ordinarily!

Immediately after the embryo transfer, the woman rests in a bed in the clinic for 3 hours. She and her husband hope that this will help encourage the embryo to implant in the uterus. After she leaves the clinic, the woman is asked to avoid heavy exercise. Some physicians also prescribe progesterone to help prepare the uterus for implantation. This drug may make a woman feel pregnant, even if she isn't. Other clinics don't prescribe any drugs at all.

The Wait

In 2 weeks, a blood test will show whether the body's hormone levels are changing in response to early pregnancy. (Although home pregnancy kits that test urine are quite accurate, this blood test is even more accurate and can be used to confirm very early pregnancy.) Although this test doesn't look at the embryo directly, a positive result confirms what is called a biochemical pregnancy. This is good, obviously, but a far more definite confirmation of pregnancy can be made 5 to 8 weeks after embryo transfer. At this stage, the fetus's heartbeat can be seen with ultrasound. The couple has achieved *clinical pregnancy*.

If a clinical pregnancy is confirmed, the couple can rejoice and prepare for a pregnancy that is subject to the same risks of miscarriage, stillbirth, and birth defects as any other pregnancy.

Unfortunately, most IVF couples will fail to have a clinical pregnancy confirmed. For reasons that still remain a challenge to fertility scientists, the embryos very often fail to implant. Of the 78 couples who have embryos transferred, only 23 couples will have their pregnancy confirmed with ultrasound. Thus, implantation occurs in just 29 percent of the women. (Twenty-nine percent of 78 couples is 23 couples.) Some experts believe this low implantation rate may also occur when eggs are fertilized naturally. No one knows for sure because under natural conditions the woman's

TABLE 1

Average Success of IVF

Cycles begun	100
Egg retrievals	87
Embryo transfers	78
Pregnancies[†]	23
Deliveries[††]	19

[†] *Pregnancies confirmed by ultrasound.*
[††] *Deliveries means number of women giving birth, not number of babies born. For example, a woman delivering triplets counts as one delivery, not three.*

monthly period begins on time or just a few days late, so she never realizes that fertilization occurred.

Fertility clinics that wish to boast of many IVF successes may define a successful IVF cycle as one that achieves a pregnancy confirmed by ultrasound. This would give them a success rate of 23 percent, well above the national average. This is misleading, however, as miscarriage is still quite likely. Miscarriage often happens in the first months of pregnancy, regardless of how the egg was fertilized. Thanks to the careful monitoring that IVF couples receive, fertility specialists know that miscarriage occurs in 19 percent of IVF pregnancies. Some experts believe miscarriage is more likely with IVF, perhaps due to the same factors that caused infertility in the first place.

Of the 23 couples who had their pregnancy confirmed with ultrasound, 4 (19 percent) will suffer a miscarriage. The remaining 19 couples will see the pregnancy carried to term and their baby born. These 19 new families represent the 19 percent IVF success rate. See Table 1.

The most useful clinical statistics describe success in terms of pregnancies that result in healthy babies rather than pregnancies achieved. If twins or triplets are born, as they are in 30 percent of IVF births, that should count in the statistics as one IVF success, not two or three.

GIFT: A Variation on In Vitro Fertilization

GIFT, which stands for *gamete intrafallopian transfer*, is another form of assisted reproductive technology. It offers a treatment option for infertile couples in which the woman has at least one open fallopian tube. Women with two blocked or damaged tubes cannot benefit from GIFT.

Instead of bringing the eggs and sperm together for fertilization in the lab, GIFT involves collecting the eggs and sperm and combining them in the fallopian tubes. Thus fertilization, if it occurs, takes place in the body rather than in the laboratory. As with natural conception, fertilization with GIFT occurs in the fallopian tubes and then the embryo travels to the uterus for implantation.

GIFT was developed in 1984 by Ricardo H. Asch at the University of Texas Health Science Center for women with at least one open tube in an effort to improve IVF's poor rate of embryo implantation. GIFT is also an alternative for couples whose religious beliefs forbid conception outside of the body.

Like IVF, GIFT allows sperm to bypass the hazardous journey through the cervix and uterus before meeting the egg. GIFT has been recommended to couples with ovulation problems, cervical mucus incompatibility, mild male infertility, and unexplained infertility. As with some uses of IVF, controversy surrounds the effectiveness of GIFT for certain forms of infertility.

The GIFT procedure is identical to IVF at the start of the cycle. The woman takes fertility drugs to stimulate the development of multiple eggs and the eggs are retrieved when they are mature. Now comes the major difference between GIFT and IVF. Once the eggs have been analyzed, a sperm sample is collected through mastrubation and washed, the physician deposits the eggs and sperm in a fallopian tube *before* fertilization.

While the woman is sedated under general anesthesia, the physician makes a small incision in the abdomen. With the use of a laparoscope, the doctor delivers the eggs and sperm into the fallopian tubes. If the woman has two unblocked tubes, some gametes are delivered to each tube. If she has only one unblocked tube, they are delivered only to that tube.

When the operation is over, the GIFT couple, like the IVF couple, must wait several weeks before the woman can have her blood tested for signs of pregnancy.

GIFT is done far less frequently than IVF. In 1994, 26,961 IVF cycles were begun but only 4,214 GIFT cycles were started. Not every fertility clinic believes that GIFT is effective. Some believe it is no more successful than intrauterine insemination. Some large fertility clinics have stopped performing GIFT procedures.

ZIFT: A Variation on GIFT

More rarely, a physician may recommend *zygote intrafallopian transfer* (*ZIFT*) to a couple. The main difference between ZIFT and GIFT is that a zygote—rather than sperm and eggs—is placed in the fallopian tube. Like IVF, the couple must wait several days after egg retrieval for the embryo to grow and divide before returning to the clinic for embryo transfer. Unlike IVF, the embryo is placed inside the fallopian tube by laparoscopy rather than into the uterus via a catheter.

ZIFT has one important advantage over GIFT: it allows the physician to learn whether the sperm are capable of fertilizing the eggs. ZIFT is done even less frequently than GIFT and its use is declining. Only 926 ZIFT procedures were performed in 1994.

TABLE 2

Success Rates of IVF, GIFT, and ZIFT

	IVF	GIFT	ZIFT
Cycles begun	26,961	4,214	926
Egg retrievals	23,254	3,692	800
Embryo/gamete transfers	20,979	3,658	696
Pregnancies[†]	6,114	1,342	278
Deliveries[††]	4,912	1,054	233
Success Rate[†††]	18.2%	25.0%	25.2%

[†] *Pregnancies confirmed by ultrasound.*

[††] *Deliveries means number of women giving birth, not number of babies born. For example, a woman delivering triplets counts as one delivery, not three.*

[†††] *The success rate is defined as percentage of deliveries per initiated cycle.*

The Statistics

Each year, statistics on IVF and other assisted reproductive methods are published in the medical journal *Fertility and Sterility.* The statistics report a variety of information, including numbers of procedures started and numbers of women giving birth. The statistics are gathered by the Society for Assisted Reproductive Technology, an organization to which most fertility clinics belong.

In 1996, the society published the data shown in Table 2 for procedures performed in the United States and Canada in 1994. The procedures were performed from January 1 to December 31, so the babies conceived with laboratory help were born from summer 1994 to fall 1995.

In comparing the success rate of these three procedures,

keep in mind that different fertility problems are treated by each of these methods. A woman with blocked fallopian tubes cannot benefit from GIFT or ZIFT, for instance.

Micromanipulation

The biggest problem with IVF—the stage at which most couples face disappointment—is embryo implantation. This is where IVF most often fails. In an effort to improve the odds that IVF will be successful, some leading embryologists began experimenting with techniques designed to encourage implantation. They wondered if slicing a hole in the outer layer of a fertilized egg would help it implant.

These pioneering experiments were conducted beginning about 1989. The embryologists who try such novel techniques—people like Jacques Cohen at St. Barnabas Medical Center in Livingston, New Jersey; Alan Handyside at Hammersmith Hospital near London; and Alan Trounson at Monash University in Melbourne, Australia—are among the leaders in the field of in vitro fertilization These medical scientists, located at a handful of laboratories around the world, design experiments aimed at improving the success of IVF.

To determine the safety of their experiments on embryos, the embryologists first try their techniques on eggs and embryos donated by infertile couples for infertility research. Once the experts perfect the new methods, other clinics adopt them and they quickly gain widespread acceptance. In 1994, about 21 percent of the IVF cycles included *micromanipulation*.

Micromanipulation, also called *microsurgery*, is performed while looking through a microscope at eggs or sperm placed in a laboratory dish or on a glass slide with a well in the center. The embryologists who do microsurgery use tiny glass pipettes and stainless steel needles to manipulate the eggs and sperm. In most cases, they craft the tools themselves. Since their own hands are far too clumsy to maneuver an egg the size of a pinprick, or a single sperm cell, which is even smaller, they rely on special instruments to help them steer their tiny tools. Practicing the necessary hand motions is crucial.

Assisted Hatching

To implant successfully, an embryo must first shed its outer layer, or zona pellucida. Embryologists who prepared embryos for transfer into the uterus noticed that women whose embryos had a thick zona seemed to have a lower rate of implantation. They wondered whether putting a small slit in the zona might actually help embryos implant. But they also worried that such an incision could have a bad effect, perhaps allowing cells in the mother's immune system to attack the embryo.

To encourage the embryo to implant, researchers developed a technique called *assisted hatching*. This technique involved making a small hole in the zona pellucida. The first clinical trials in assisted hatching, also known as partial zona dissection, were conducted by embryologist Jacques Cohen while he was at New York Hospital-Cornell Medical Center and, working separately, by a team in Israel in 1989 and 1990.

In these small trials, assisted hatching appeared to benefit women over age 38 and women who had failed to achieve pregnancy after previous cycles of IVF. Slowly, assisted hatching spread to a few other IVF centers with embryologists experienced enough to offer the procedure. Some clinics adopted assisted hatching as standard practice for women over age 40 and women whose embryos had thick zona pellucidas.

Assisted hatching begins by capturing the egg and holding it steady with a tiny glass pipette. Once the egg is secure, the embryologist cuts a small slit in the zona pellucida with a sharp instrument, like an injection needle. Medical scientists have also used lasers and chemicals to cut the zona.

Assisted hatching has its risks. Apparently the embryo can get squeezed while emerging from the shell and create two genetically identical individuals. In 1994, the team at New York Hospital-Cornell Medical Center publicly speculated in a medical journal that six cases of identical twins born after assisted hatching suggested that an unintended side effect of the procedure might be identical twins.[4]

More worrisome was a report from the same team a year later in another medical journal stating that assisted hatching had almost certainly been responsible for creating a triplet pregnancy that included twins connected at the trunk: *conjoined*—or Siamese—twins, in other words. Those twins were aborted early in pregnancy. [5]

Reports like these serve as stern warnings that experimental techniques cannot be considered safe on the basis of a small number of healthy births. Certain hazards or side effects may become evident only after a large group of births is studied. Ethically, infertile couples must be notified of all risks as they consider any assisted reproductive technique. They cannot be said to have given their informed consent until they know about and accept all potential risks. In the United States, the reporting of harmful side effects depends on the professionalism and sense of obligation of the scientists involved.

Intracytoplasmic Sperm Injection

Although IVF was first developed to treat women with blocked or missing fallopian tubes, fertility experts soon realized that, in some cases, it seems to offer benefits to men with sperm defects. That's because IVF requires far fewer healthy sperm to fertilize an egg than does normal fertilization. Still, fertility specialists had no solution for couples whose eggs refused to fertilize during IVF. What was needed was a way to place a single healthy sperm directly into the egg itself.

Embryologists began experimenting with inserting

sperm into the area between the zona and the egg. This was called *subzonal sperm insertion* (*SUZI*) and had only limited success. But a more successful method of sperm injection was developed by Belgian physician Gianpiero D. Palermo. His technique, perfected at a clinic in Brussels, Belgium, involves injecting a sperm cell directly into the egg.

Palermo's method is known as intracytoplasmic sperm injection. Today, ICSI is used to achieve pregnancy in the partners of men with severe sperm defects, including sperm with poor movement or sperm that lack the ability to penetrate an egg.

The first baby conceived with help from ICSI was born in Belgium in 1992. The sperm injection technique was introduced to the United States in 1993 by the Genetics & IVF Institute of Fairfax, Virginia, which achieved the first American ICSI pregnancies. Soon after, Palermo moved to New York Hospital-Cornell Medical Center and taught the technique to other embryologists there. The method, hailed as a medical breakthrough, spread quickly.

With ICSI, the IVF cycle is essentially the same: ovaries are stimulated with drugs; eggs are retrieved, fertilized, and incubated; and embryos are transferred. ICSI simply adds an additional step. After the eggs have been removed from the woman and the sperm have been washed, the embryologist selects the most active sperm and takes steps to slow them down so that they're easier to manipulate. This is done by dunking them in a special solution. Once a single sperm has been chosen, the embryologist pinches its whiplike tail to immobilize it and keep it from causing damage inside the egg.

The embryologist holds one egg at a time with a pipette and pierces its zona pellucida with a needle or other instrument. The sperm is injected into the center of the egg with a pipette. If all goes well, the genetic material of the gametes will combine. This step takes less than a minute. Sound easy? Sperm injection actually requires experienced embryologists who have practiced on hamster eggs until they have perfected the tiny, precise movements needed to perform the procedure.

As you learned in Chapter 3, ICSI is often used to achieve pregnancy in the partners of men with severe sperm defects. This procedure makes it possible to fertilize an egg with sperm that have poor mobility or lack the ability to penetrate an egg. The sperm used for this type of ICSI is obtained through masturbation.

Some men manufacture plenty of healthy sperm in their testes, but ejaculate semen that contains no sperm at all. This is because their sperm ducts are blocked. Although physicians have known how to remove immature sperm from the testes for several years, immature sperm are incapable of penetrating and fertilizing an egg. ICSI offers a solution to this problem. ICSI with immature sperm also allows men with spinal cord injuries to father children. Although these men are capable of producing normal sperm, their injury prevents ejaculation.

The main difference between standard IVF and IVF with sperm injection, of course, is that the IVF cycle with sperm injection is being done solely to treat *male* infertility. The fertile female partner agrees to the drug treatment and invasive techniques of IVF out of a strong desire to have a baby with her partner's sperm.

Culturing Immature Eggs
Because infertility drugs may cause uncomfortable side effects or disrupt implantation, fertility scientists have been trying to develop a technique that would eliminate the need for fertility drugs in the IVF cycle. They would like to be able to identify and remove tiny immature eggs from the ovaries and then mature them in the laboratory before fertilization. (Fertility drugs, remember, are used to make many eggs mature at once.) Using immature eggs would also eliminate the need for daily monitoring and meticulously timing the retrieval of the eggs before ovulation.

Using the newest ultrasound equipment, scientists can

locate immature eggs in tiny follicles less than 1/10-inch (0.25-mm) wide. Scientists have also been experimenting with incubating eggs in various growth media.

The culturing of immature eggs has already produced a handful of births. It was first used by Kwang Yul Cha and his colleagues at the Cha Women's Hospital in Seoul, South Korea, in 1991. The woman who underwent IVF with immature eggs gave birth to triplets.

The technique was also used successfully by Australia's Alan Trounson. His first successful patient, Robyn Hallam, agreed to the experiment because past attempts at IVF had failed. She was quoted in *Time* as saying: "What do we have to lose?" [6] After Trounson cultured and fertilized her immature eggs and transferred the embryos to her body, she gave birth to a daughter, Kezia Hallam, on December 14, 1993. Despite these early successes, culturing immature eggs for in vitro fertilization is still an experiment that only a few clinics are investigating.

Preimplantation Genetic Diagnosis

In 1990, Alan Handyside of Hammersmith Hospital, outside London, reported that he had successfully removed one cell from an eight-celled embryo without interfering with the normal development of the embryo.[7] By conducting a DNA test on that one cell, scientists now had a way to determine if the embryo was male or female. More sophisticated testing could identify whether or not the embryo carried a genetic disease.

Preimplantation genetic diagnosis has been used by couples whose children are at risk for serious, life-threatening genetic diseases. Although this procedure is unrelated to fertility treatment, the development of IVF made preimplantation genetic diagnosis possible. With preimplantation genetic diagnosis, couples can have their embryos tested, so that only the unaffected embryos will be transferred to the woman's uterus. Any affected embryos are destroyed. This prenatal test is similar, in theory, to other types of genetic tests done on the fetus during pregnancy. The big difference, of course, is that if an affected fetus is identified during pregnancy, the parents must abort the pregnancy if they wish to avoid having an affected baby.

In the few years since Handyside's report, prenatal diagnostic testing has been used to detect genetic diseases like cystic fibrosis and Tay-Sachs disease. It has also been used to identify male embryos at risk for sex-linked diseases like hemophilia, a blood-clotting disorder, and Duchenne muscular dystrophy. A woman at risk for giving birth to a son with a sex-linked disease can request that only female embryos be transferred to her uterus. To date, most couples requesting the procedure have already seen one or more of their children sicken or die from a genetic disease.

Some ethicists fear that this kind of prenatal test might some day enable people to shop for the perfect baby. Could preimplantation genetic diagnosis be used one day to select an embryo that is destined to be tall, smart, and athletically talented? Critics worry that the conception laboratory will become a place where would-be parents can make requests about their baby's physical appearance and personality, as well as physical health. This is far in the future, however, as preinplantation diagnosis is only available at the most advanced, state-of-the-art fertility clinics in the world.

Other kinds of prenatal tests have become an accepted part of medical practice. Should preimplantation genetic diagnosis really be regarded differently? Perhaps, since it eliminates entirely the role of abortion. On the other hand, it requires IVF, an expensive and invasive procedure. It's difficult to imagine people who are not at risk for a serious disease willing to undergo IVF simply for trait selection.

6

BABIES
WITH
THREE
"PARENTS"

In vitro fertilization makes it possible for a woman to give birth to a child who is not, genetically speaking, her own. With the arrival of IVF, medical science found it had the means to split motherhood two ways: one woman could provide the egg for fertilization in the lab and a second woman could carry the embryo to term. The woman who intended to raise the child—its social and legal mother—could be either the woman donating the egg or the woman providing the uterus. In theory, it could even be a different, third woman.

Alan Trounson, the Australian fertility expert, was the first embryologist to transfer a donated egg during an IVF cycle and see a successful pregnancy follow. The birth that resulted from that cycle took place in Melbourne in November 1983.[1] A girl born at Mt. Sinai Medical Center in Cleveland on April 13, 1986, was heralded by *The New York Times* as the first American baby born from a host uterus.[2] By 1990, about 300 children conceived with donated eggs had been born worldwide.

The use of donated eggs or a host uterus is still quite rare. In 1994, 3,119 cycles with donated eggs were begun in the United States and 929 women gave birth. That same year, 219 cycles with a host uterus were begun and 56 women gave birth. As with standard IVF, these procedures resulted in many multiple births.

From a medical standpoint, including donated eggs or a volunteer uterus in an IVF cycle was only slightly more difficult than running an ordinary IVF cycle. Most of the challenge lay in the need to synchronize the menstrual cycles of the two women involved. From every other standpoint, however, contracting women for the use of their eggs or their wombs represented an enormous leap into a brave new world. Socially, legally, and psychologically, this use of medical technology has proven to be quite daunting. Although these procedures are heavily promoted by certain clinics in the United States, they are prohibited or simply not offered in many parts of the world.

Who Uses Donated Eggs?

Women who are unable to produce good quality eggs, perhaps because of age or ovarian problems, very often still have healthy wombs. They are able to accept an embryo transfer and carry a pregnancy to term. The same is true for women who have no eggs at all due to premature menopause or radiation treatment for cancer. A woman at risk for passing on an inherited disease may also elect not to conceive a child with her own eggs. Even women in their late 40s and 50s, who are past normal menopause, have become pregnant this way. With eggs donated by a volunteer and fertilized with sperm from their partners, such women are able to become pregnant and experience giving birth. Although they lack a genetic connection to the baby, their partner is the baby's biological father.

The decision to use donated eggs is a very difficult one. If the woman is producing eggs of her own, a couple may

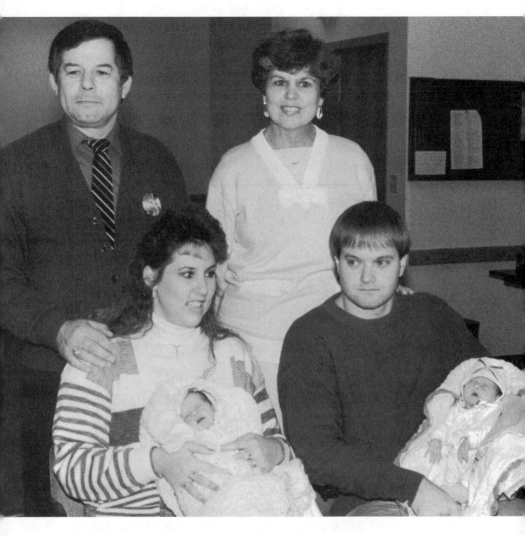

Woman Gives Birth to Own Grandchildren—that's what the headlines said when Arlette Schweitzer (top right) gave birth to twins that were the product of her daughter's egg and her son-in-law's sperm. Arlette acted as the host uterus for her daughter, who was born without a uterus. Here, Arlette and her husband, Dan (top left), pose with their daughter, Christa Uchytil, their son-in-law, Kevin Uchytil, and babies Chelsea and Chad.

hold out hope that they can conceive a child together. This is especially true for women over age 35 whose only impediment to fertility is advancing age. The couple may spend several years and many thousands of dollars on IVF and other treatments before letting go of that dream. They may seriously consider adoption before deciding to attempt pregnancy with donated eggs.

With adoption, neither parent has a genetic link to the baby. Some couples may feel that this is important, since both parents would be on the same footing when it comes to a biological link to the child. With egg donation, only the mother gives up a genetic tie. Egg donation may also have less to offer couples of certain ethnic backgrounds. Eggs from African-American or Jewish donors, for example, are in extremely short supply.

Couples who ultimately choose to pursue egg donation may see advantages over adoption. With adoption, they may fear a custody claim from the birth parents. They may worry about whether the birth mother received proper prenatal care. Egg donation allows the couple to share the experience of pregnancy and birth together. The cost of private adoption and egg donation are comparable, about $15,000 to $20,000 or more.

Who Uses a Host Uterus?

A host uterus is one solution for a woman who ovulates normally each month but is unable to carry a pregnancy to term. It may be that she repeatedly miscarries. Or her uterus may have defects from exposure to diethylstilbestrol. Perhaps the problem is the result of a medical condition such as multiple sclerosis or diabetes. She may even have been born without a uterus or illness may have required the surgical removal of her uterus.

With IVF, the infertile woman and her partner can create embryos in the laboratory and then have them transferred into the uterus of another woman. This woman provides the host uterus. She carries the fetus and gives birth, but she is not the source of the egg that produced the child. At birth, the second woman relinquishes the baby to the couple who provided the gametes for its conception. The woman who carries the pregnancy in this instance is sometimes called a *gestational surrogate mother.*

Coordinating Egg Retrieval and Embryo Transfer

Unlike sperm and even embryos, eggs cannot be frozen and thawed successfully. For this reason, eggs intended for donation or transfer into a host uterus must be fresh. This means that when the first woman's ovaries are ready for egg retrieval, the second woman's uterus must be ready for embryo transfer 2 or 3 days later. To ensure this careful coordination, the fertility clinic synchronizes the women's menstrual cycles by first stopping them with drugs, and then starting them again at the same time. The woman producing the eggs also receives ovarian-stimulating drugs so that she produces multiple eggs. The woman receiving the eggs may be given progesterone after the transfer to encourage her uterus to accept the embryo.

In all other respects, the procedure resembles a normal IVF cycle. Multiple eggs are retrieved from the woman supplying the eggs and fertilized in the lab with the sperm of the intended father. After 2 or 3 days, if some of the eggs have been fertilized successfully, the four- or eight-cell embryos are transferred into the woman who will carry the pregnancy. Compared to IVF, these procedures also have a higher rate of success. About 30 percent of the women who begin an IVF cycle with donor eggs will give birth, according to the most recent statistics. The success rate with host uterus is about 26 percent.

In the case of donated eggs, the two women involved need never meet. In the use of a host uterus, the intended couple will almost certainly have contact with the gestational surrogate during pregnancy. Immediately after birth, the host surrogate releases the baby to them.

Third-Party Conception

Using donated eggs or a host uterus is sometimes called third-party conception because the infertile couple is involving a third person in their efforts to reproduce. Other forms of third-party conception include *traditional surrogate* motherhood and the use of donor sperm. All third-party methods of conception share some similarities, certainly. The ethical issues they raise overlap. But they also differ in important ways.

Surrogate Motherhood
Surrogate motherhood is available, in some parts of the world, to couples faced with female infertility. The man and woman seek another woman to become inseminated with the man's sperm and to carry the resulting pregnancy. Surrogacy in this form has existed for centuries. The Bible contains the story of how Sarah offered her husband her maid, Hagar, to bear the children she could not conceive. Abraham and Sarah's son Ishmael was born as a result of Abraham's union with Hagar (Genesis 16: 1–4). Surrogate motherhood has changed little since biblical times, except that today medically assisted insemination has replaced sexual intercourse.

More than 8,000 children have been born in the United States this way. If all goes as planned, the surrogate mother relinquishes the newborn baby created with her egg and the intended father's sperm to the couple. The child is raised by its biological father and his wife, the intended mother. The man's wife is not genetically related to the child and must adopt the baby through a stepparent adoption. For her services, the surrogate mother receives a fee, usually between $10,000 and $15,000.[3]

94

Surrogate motherhood almost always goes smoothly. The surrogate reports a tremendous feeling of satisfaction while the new parents express gratitude. It is not unusual for the surrogate mother to remain a part of the baby's life through birthday cards, letters, and even occasional visits. However the complicated legal and moral issues involved have prompted a number of countries worldwide and states in the United States to make the practice illegal.

The highly publicized Baby M case of 1987, in which surrogate mother Mary Beth Whitehead sought custody of the baby she carried for William and Elizabeth Stern, served to underscore how vulnerable everyone involved is to deep feelings of pain if things go awry. Whitehead eventually gained visitation rights, but not custody.

Although surrogate motherhood hardly seems "traditional," it is sometimes called traditional surrogate motherhood to distinguish it from gestational surrogate motherhood. It can also be referred to as genetic surrogate motherhood or contract motherhood.

Couples seeking the services of a traditional surrogate often contact agencies that maintain lists of women willing to be surrogates. Often, the services of these women are also available to couples seeking a host surrogate to carry their embryo. Typically, surrogate mothers are married with children of their own. They usually don't work outside the home and have a high school education. They are willing to become surrogates because they enjoy pregnancy and wish to help someone else create a family. Occasionally, host surrogates are relatives of the infertile couple.

Although traditional surrogates and host surrogates may come from the same agency, two important differences distinguish the two types of surrogacy. First, in traditional surrogacy, the woman who carries the baby also provides the egg that creates the baby. She has a genetic connection to the child. In gestational surrogacy, the woman carrying the baby has no genetic connection to the child.

The second difference is that pregnancy in traditional surrogacy is achieved by inseminating the surrogate mother with the intended father's sperm. The sperm sample is obtained through masturbation. Assisted insemination is usually done by a physician although insemination at home, with a sterile plastic syringe, is also possible. Gestational surrogacy, on the other hand, involves transferring embryos created by the gametes of the intended parents. Gestational surrogacy is a more expensive and complicated procedure that includes IVF and the skills of highly trained fertility specialists.

In host surrogacy, unlike traditional surrogacy, couples may be able to sidestep adoption proceedings after the baby's birth. In California, where several agencies have flourished, it is possible to list the name of the genetic mother on the birth certificate along with the name of her partner, the genetic father. (Ordinarily, the name of the woman giving birth is the name listed on the birth certificate.) To do this, an attorney must appear in court to receive an order from a judge directing the hospital to fill out the birth certificate with the name of the genetic mother, rather than the host mother.

Use of Donor Sperm

Insemination with sperm from a donor is one option available to couples faced with male infertility. In this procedure, the intended mother is inseminated with donor sperm obtained from a commercial sperm bank. The sperm costs between $125 and $250 per sample. More than 30,000 babies are conceived in this way each year.

The sperm donor's identity typically remains unknown to the infertile couple. (For this reason, the donor is sometimes referred to as an anonymous donor.) The woman carries the baby and gives birth just as if she achieved pregnancy in the usual way. For decades, physicians counseled couples to keep their baby's origins a secret. In recent years, there has been a move toward more openness.

IN THE NEWS

Pregnancies that include donor eggs or a host uterus were brand-new in the early 1990s and made frequent headlines. Some stories that were covered in the popular press include:

"All in the Family."
By Nash, J. Madeline.
Time. August 19, 1991, p. 58.

At 42, Arlette Schweitzer, of Aberdeen, South Dakota, provided her daughter with a host uterus to carry the twins conceived with her daughter's eggs and her son-in-law's sperm. (See photo, p. 91)

"Turning Back the Biological Clock."
By Rosen, Marjorie.
People Weekly. November 12, 1990, p. 115.

One woman's story of giving birth after early menopause with a donated egg.

"Ruth Pointer Gives Birth to In-Vitro Twins."
Ebony. November 1993, p. 122.

At the age of 47, soul singer Ruth Pointer gave birth to twins. The twins were conceived with donated eggs and the sperm of Pointer's husband. Pointer had three other children and two grandchildren at the time of the birth.

"Old Enough to Be Your Mother."
By Carlson, Margaret.
Time. January 10, 1994, p. 41.

Should women past menopause use IVF and donor eggs to give birth? This article examines the controversy.

Use of Donor Eggs

About 20 percent of egg donations involve a donor who is a sister or close friend of the infertile woman. The remaining 80 percent involve a donor who is a stranger to the infertile couple and who is paid $1,500 to $3,000 for her services.

Ads for egg donors have begun cropping up in college newspapers across the United States. In the University of Washington student newspaper, this ad appeared recently: "Egg donors needed to help infertile women at the University of Washington Fertility and Endocrine Center. Must be 21 to 34, have a history of pregnancy, be celibate or in a monogamous, long-term relationship and have a minimum of one year of college. $1,700 reimbursement." In the *Daily Bruin,* the student paper of the University of California, Los Angeles, another ad read: "Egg donors desperately wanted by infertile, hopeful parents. All races needed. Ages 21 to 30. Compensation $3,000."

Ads like these speak to the high demand for women who are willing to become egg donors. The ads are placed by fertility clinics or by donor brokers, people who bring egg donors and infertile couples together for a fee of several thousand dollars. More rarely, couples place the ads themselves.

College students have been targeted as potential donors, in all likelihood because they are young, smart, and presumably strapped for cash. But is that all it takes to become an egg donor? The American Society for Reproductive Medicine has recommended that potential egg donors be healthy and younger than age 34. This reflects the fact that the eggs of a woman age 35 and older are at a higher risk of producing a child with a chromosomal abnormality like Down syndrome. The ASRM standards also recommend that egg donors show evidence of fertility, having had either an abortion or children.[4]

Although commercial egg donation is still very new, several observations have been made about the women who have stepped forward as donors. While egg donors expect payment for their time and the discomfort they undergo, money is usually not their sole motivation. Women who donate eggs often do so out of a strong desire to help someone else become a mother.

They may have witnessed a friend or family member struggle with infertility. Their own children may be so central to their lives that they wish to make that joy possible for someone else. In some instances, women have become egg donors as a way of making peace with themselves after an abortion. Occasionally, women will donate the extra eggs produced while going through IVF themselves.

Once a potential egg donor meets the clinic's or broker's minimum requirements for participation, her medical history is carefully reviewed. A woman whose offspring are at risk for an inherited disease are eliminated from further consideration. The ASRM also recommends that the potential egg donor undergo screening to detect sexually transmitted diseases, including AIDS.

Psychological counseling about the effects of giving up one's genetic material is also important. Sometimes potential candidates are screened for financial stability and maturity. The clinic or broker wants to be certain that the donor will be able to follow the regimen of fertility drugs and office visits. They also want to avoid relying on any woman who seems under pressure from another person to become an egg donor. The screening process takes several appointments over a period of weeks.

Family members or friends who volunteer to become donors must go through the same process. They are also carefully interviewed to make sure they have not been coerced. The clinic wants to feel confident that the potential donor has thought through the entire process, especially her future relationship with the recipient couple and the child that will be born. She may be asked how she expects that relationship to change or how she might feel if the baby is not raised in a way she condones.

Once a donor is accepted, most clinics limit the number of times she undergoes ovarian stimulation and egg retrieval to fewer than five cycles. This serves two purposes. First, it reduces the donor's exposure to fertility drugs and the long-term cancer risk they may pose. Second, it reduces the total number of children conceived with her eggs. No one yet knows what the psychological effects will be on children when they learn that they may have four or five half-siblings living in several different families. ASRM guidelines say donors should contribute to no more than ten live births to reduce the already extremely small chance that a child would ever meet and marry half-siblings.

Closed adoption, in which the records revealing the identity of the birth mother were permanently sealed, was standard practice for years. Recently, however, evidence gathered by social workers and psychologists has demonstrated how important it can be for adopted people to know more of the facts surrounding their birth. Adult adoptees, driven to learn more about their biological parents, have successfully lobbied states to make adoption papers available to them. Open adoption, in which the birth mother and the adoptive parents meet and often maintain contact, is currently gaining acceptance.

This trend in adoption has affected egg donation as well, though the amount of contact that an egg donor and a recipient couple may have varies enormously from clinic to clinic. At clinics that promote closed donation, the egg donor's identity is carefully concealed from the recipient couple and the donor never even learns whether pregnancy was achieved with her egg. Clinics on the other end of the spectrum encourage the couple to meet their egg donor or, at the very least, to accept her photograph.

Although egg and sperm donation are similar in some respects, there are important differences. One of the most significant of these differences involves the degree of inconvenience and medical risk to the donors. Sperm donation is completed in little time and is risk-free. Egg donation, on the other hand, requires a major time commitment. It involves the use of fertility drugs, frequent trips to the doctor for monitoring, and then an invasive procedure to retrieve the eggs. The egg donor is at risk for developing drug-related side effects. For all these reasons, egg donors are typically paid several thousand dollars, while sperm donors receive $50 to $75.

Ethical Concerns

Traditional Surrogacy

The use of a traditional surrogate mother—a woman who supplies an egg and carries the pregnancy in exchange for a fee—has already been hotly debated. (Traditional surrogacy, remember, does not require in vitro fertilization.) It is unlawful in Great Britain, Israel, Germany, Sweden, and France, as well as in New Jersey, Arizona, Florida, Michigan, and Washington state.

Many opponents of surrogacy believe that it is immoral for a woman to sign an agreement to give up a child before she is even pregnant. Some people condemn surrogacy only if money changes hands. Others are willing to permit surrogacy so long as the surrogate mother has the opportunity to retain her parental rights if she changes her mind. Many of the laws written to discourage traditional surrogacy would affect gestational surrogates as well.

Egg Donation and Host Uterus

Does the practice of egg donation and host uterus (gestational surrogacy) best belong to the realm of science fiction? Babies are soft and sweet-smelling and seem the opposite, really, of futuristic technology. We're not talking about computers or robots or nuclear weapons or even artificial hearts here. Nevertheless, certain fundamental assumptions about ourselves are challenged each time a woman gives birth to a baby that has grown from the egg of another.

No one wants to add to the pain of couples struggling to resolve their infertility with these methods. But the use of donated eggs or a host uterus has the potential to create situations that seem astonishing at best, and unnatural at worst. Opponents of the practices claim that they are degrading to women and treat women like commodities. The critics wonder whether the ethical implications of these new techniques have ever been adequately examined. "The profound question is whether we treat these developments as profound or take them for granted," declared bioethicist Arthur L. Caplan in a 1993 newspaper article. [5]

In Germany and Switzerland, the use of donated eggs has been banned. In Louisiana, payment for eggs is prohibited, as it is in England. ASRM guidelines may be splitting hairs when they recommend that an egg donor be paid for her time and effort, but not her eggs.

Some critics initially worried gestational surrogacy might lead to the development of an underclass of breeders: women who make a living by carrying the embryos of rich couples. This hasn't happened, probably because most women wish to carry their babies themselves. Careful screening of potential host surrogates has also helped weed out those motivated only by money. However, unless the medical and psychological risks of their services are carefully explained, host surrogates could be easily exploited. As it is, they are almost always younger, less educated, and have lower incomes than the intended parents. Since infertile couples usually don't turn to use of a host uterus until they are in their late 30s or early 40s—when other high-tech options have failed, these differences may be impossible to avoid.

It might seem that a host surrogate—who has no genetic connection to the fetus she carries—would be unlikely to seek custody of that child once it is born. It has happened, however. In a well-publicized California case, Anna Johnson, a gestational surrogate hired to carry the embryo created with gametes from Mark and Crispina Calvert, sued for custody, child support, and emotional damages after delivering a baby boy on September 19, 1990. She declared that she had bonded with the unborn baby. On ABC's *Good Morning America*, she said, "The baby, while it's growing inside me, has my cells and my blood nurturing this child, maintaining its life." She said she had been hurt by the Calverts' inattention and late payments.

At the custody hearing, psychiatrist Michelle Harrison stated that "the Calverts are this child's link to his genetic past. Anna Johnson is his link to his human past." Harrison was a member of the National Coalition Against Surrogacy. Despite testimony from Harrison and other experts who argued that Anna's maternal bond should be honored, the court ruled against Anna on October 29. Custody of the baby was given to the Calverts.[6]

Post-Menopausal Pregnancy

Controversy has also followed the use of egg donation to achieve pregnancy in women who have gone through menopause. In 1993, several medical teams jockeyed to be the first to announce that a healthy baby conceived with a donated egg had been born to a woman older than 50.[7] Debates raged both inside and outside the medical profession. Newspaper columns appeared on both sides of the issue. Those in favor of post-menopausal birth argued that older women who wished to become pregnant had a right to control their own bodies. Besides, men in their 50s and 60s routinely fathered children. Those opposed claimed that it upset the natural life cycle and bespoke a fear of aging and death. They questioned the fairness of bringing a child into the world whose mother would be in her 60s or 70s during the child's teenage years. Not long after the discussion began, a 59-year-old British woman gave birth.

Her pregnancy and others soon after proved once and for all that a decrease in egg quality, rather than the condition of the uterus, accounts for the decreased fertility in older women. As long as the donated eggs come from young, healthy women, the risk of age-related birth defects, like Down syndrome, is low. While birth defects are no more likely than they are for younger women, carrying the fetus to term is substantially more difficult for older women.

ASRM guidelines note that various national reports have recommended limiting the age of the egg recipients to avoid extending the natural reproductive life span. In practice, this restricts the age of recipients to 50 years. Women older than 50 cannot receive eggs unless they are still menstruating naturally.

Considering the Children
Will the children who are born through arrangements involving donated eggs or surrogate mothers think of themselves as having two mothers, as adopted children do? How will this affect their sense of identity? These questions will remain unanswered until the first wave of babies, born in the late 1980s, grow up.

7

TOO

MANY

EMBRYOS,

TOO MANY

BABIES

When humans are born in pairs, the twins attract an extra dollop of attention from friends and family. When babies are born in sets of three or four or five, the world sits up and takes notice. Multiple births, especially quadruplets and quintuplets, make headline news. Newspaper photos show the parents looking weary but triumphant. The medical team boasts of its success. Local businesses step forward and pledge to supply the family with pizza or diapers or baby food for a year.

One of the most significant risks of fertility treatment—certainly the one with the farthest-reaching consequences and the one that has the most impact on society's resources—is multiple births. For a couple who has been unable to produce even a single baby after years of trying, such ready-made families can sound mighty appealing. Yet while twins, triplets, and more create excitement and interest, they also create a multitude of problems. The use of fertility drugs, either alone or in combination with in vitro fertilization, is directly responsible for the recent phenomenal rise in multiple births.

The reality of multiple births is much starker than sugar-coated news stories admit. Babies born as multiples are seven times more likely to die in the first 28 days of life than single babies. They are very often born prematurely—before they are fully developed. More than half weigh less than 5.5 pounds (2.5 kg) at birth, and some weigh much less. (Five-and-a-half pounds [2.5 kg] is considered the bottom end of the normal range of birth weight.)

Because the lungs of these premature babies are often not fully developed, many must spend their first weeks attached to a respirator to help them breathe. Many premature babies face weeks of intensive care in the hospital. A plastic incubator may help keep their body temperature up, but it is no substitute for their mother's womb. Many develop multiple handicaps, including blindness, cerebral palsy, and mental retardation.

Carrying two or more babies is also harder on the mother than carrying just one. Many multiple babies require a cesarean-section delivery. In this operation, the babies are delivered through a surgical incision in the abdomen. Cesarean deliveries have a slightly higher rate of complications than normal deliveries. Women pregnant with multiples also are more likely to develop high blood pressure and anemia during pregnancy. These conditions can, in turn, make for a more difficult birth and recovery for the mother. Too much bleeding, known as hemorrhage, is another hazard of delivering multiples.

The costs associated with multiple births can be astronomical. The cost of delivering a single baby is about $5,000, while the average cost of delivering triplets is $64,000. A 1994 report examining 6 years of births at Brigham and Women's Hospital in Boston concluded that if all multiple births resulting from fertility drugs, IVF, GIFT, and ZIFT had been single births instead, the savings to the

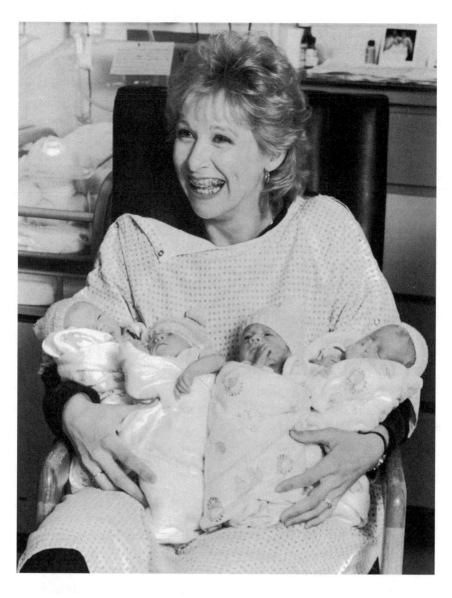

At one time, Dixie Schock of Gillette, Wyoming thought she might never have children. Here she is shown with her 2-week-old quadruplets—Ryan, Ashley, Colton, and Amber.

health-care system in the hospital would have been more than $3 million per year.[1]

Caring for several infants or several toddlers is a marathon of exhaustion that runs round the clock. Families faced with the challenging task of raising triplets are very likely to show stress and depression, according to medical studies.[2] One parent cannot give adequate attention to all three children. The family may feel unable to leave the house because of the difficulties in going out and the stares from strangers. Finances may be quickly drained. For local businesses, the novelty of giving free gifts may soon wear off. Parents cannot count on free giveaways as they raise their growing family. Such stresses of parenting often lead to child abuse. Sadly, such abuse is more common in families with multiples than in families where children arrived one at a time.

In the early 1900s, twins occurred once in ninety births and other multiples, like triplets or quadruplets, were practically unheard of. When the Dionne quintuplets were born in 1934, they were treated by the Canadian government like a wonder of the world. Today, multiples occur once in every forty births. The majority of those births are twins, but each year, 2,500 sets of triplets are born. In 1996, the United States had forty-two living sets of quintuplets. The birth rate of higher-order multiples—triplets, quadruplets, and the like—almost tripled in the 13 years between 1980 and 1993.[3]

Some of the increase in multiples—about 30 percent— is due to the large number of mothers over age 35 giving birth. (Although women older than 35 are less likely to conceive than younger women, they are more likely to ovulate more than one egg at a time.) Improvements in the care of premature babies also accounts for the increased likelihood of survival among multiple babies. The rest, however, is directly related to fertility treatment.

Since more than one fertilized egg is transferred during assisted reproduction, you might expect those techniques to produce multiple births—and they do. Techniques like IVF

TABLE 3

Odds of Multiple Births

	Twins	Triplets	Quadruplets
Natural rate	1 in 90	1 in 10,000	1 in 600,000
IVF pregnancy	1 in 4	1 in 20	1 in 200
GIFT pregnancy	1 in 4	1 in 14	1 in 200

and GIFT are responsible for about 38 percent of multiple births, but another 32 percent is due to the use of fertility drugs alone. The rate of multiple births is 1 in 10 for women using clomiphene only and 1 in 5 for women using hMG only. Fertility drugs stimulate the ovaries to produce several eggs and, quite often, if pregnancy occurs, more than one of those eggs will be fertilized.

If fertility drugs and assisted reproduction resulted only in a greater chance of having twins, it's hard to imagine many parents or physicians complaining. The most serious problems—medical and otherwise—occur with triplets and on up. With high-tech procedures, however, they occur much more frequently.

The data for IVF and GIFT pregnancies in Table 3 were collected by the American Society for Reproductive Medicine for the year 1994. The data reflect only actual multiple babies born. (Those selectively reduced by abortion are not included.)

The Sad Case of the Frustaci Septuplets

The fertility drug Pergonal (brand name for hMG) has become infamous for its potential to create high numbers of multiple births thanks to several pregnancies that led to lawsuits and extensive media coverage. One of these was the sad story of Patricia Frustaci and her husband Samuel. In 1984, they sought the services of fertility doctor Jaroslav Marik and the Tyler Medical Clinic in Westwood, California, for infertility treatment. Pergonal was prescribed, and Frustaci became pregnant with seven babies. Seven babies cannot be born healthy. Some are likely to die before or during birth. The odds against even one healthy baby surviving are high.

Frustaci's doctors advised her to terminate the pregnancy with abortion or to at least abort most of the fetuses. But Frustaci, a member of the Mormon faith, refused. She was morally opposed to abortion. She was told that if she continued to carry the pregnancy, none of the babies might survive. By aborting some of the fetuses, she might be able to deliver one or two healthy babies. She remained unswayed by this argument. She spent the last months of her pregnancy in St. Joseph's Hospital in Orange, California. News photos showed her lying in a hospital bed, facedown, with her belly protruding through a hole specially cut for it.

On May 22, 1985, Frustaci delivered four boys and three girls. One was stillborn. Three more infants died in the days and months that followed. The three survivors suffered from cerebral palsy. Frustaci and her husband sued the clinic. Testimony revealed that either Frustaci's dosage was improperly monitored by the clinic or she intentionally took too much of the drug. In July 1990, Tyler Medical Clinic agreed to pay up to $6 million spread over the lifetime of the three surviving children to settle the lawsuit. At the time the settlement was announced, Patti Frustaci was pregnant with twins, again after taking Pergonal.[5]

Cases like the Frustaci septuplets have grown rare, thankfully. But headlines announcing a pregnancy in which the woman is carrying seven or even eight fetuses still appear regularly. Although the pregnancies sound like they must have involved some high-tech medical involvement, they are almost certainly the unfortunate result of fertility drugs alone. Assisted reproductive procedures, like IVF or

GIFT, can result in quadruplets or quintuplets only if more than three embryos are transferred and all develop.

A Difficult Choice

Fetal reduction—also known as selective reduction or selective abortion—was developed in the early 1980s in response to the problem of a pregnancy with many fetuses. It was the imperfect solution offered to Patti Frustaci.

In those rare cases when four or more embryos implant and begin to develop, parents and doctors are shocked and dismayed. After finally achieving a dearly-wished-for pregnancy, the couple learns that the odds of delivering even one healthy baby are very small.

Should the parents continue the pregnancy? The multiple pregnancy threatens the health of the mother and may result in no babies or babies with severe handicaps. Should they abort the pregnancy? That would mean destroying what they had tried so long and so hard to create. Both choices seem equally unacceptable. Aborting some, but not all, of the fetuses may be a way of avoiding this impossible decision.

In the late 1970s and early 1980s, doctors began to wonder whether a multiple pregnancy could be reduced to twins or triplets. No one knew for sure. In the United States, abortion was legal and so, clearly, was selective abortion. But could it be done? Should it be done? Would the remaining, unharmed fetuses continue to develop?

The first fetal reduction was performed in Europe. Soon after, the procedure became available in the United States. At first, the doctors did their work quietly to avoid publicity. They knew they were potential targets of the strong anti-abortion movement.

Among the pioneers of this practice were Richard Berkowitz at Mt. Sinai Medical Center in New York City, Mark I. Evans at Wayne State University's Hutzel Hospital in Detroit, and Ronald J. Wapner of Jefferson Medical College in Philadelphia. For the most part, practitioners of fetal reduction learned the procedure on their own after hearing that it had been done successfully elsewhere.

Although the decision to reduce a pregnancy may be extremely difficult emotionally, fetal reduction itself is relatively simple. It is performed at about 10 weeks, when the fetuses are about 1.5 inches (3.8 cm) long. Using ultrasound, the doctor locates the fetuses and guides a needle through the woman's abdomen and into the chest of the closest fetus. The physician then injects potassium chloride into the fetus. The drug stops the fetus's heart and the fetus dies. About 20 percent of the time, the entire pregnancy miscarries. The rest of the time, the other fetuses continue to grow and the dead fetus is absorbed by the body.

Predictably, couples with a pregnancy of four or more fetuses are more likely to seek fetal reduction than those expecting triplets. Although most physicians who perform reductions are willing to reduce a pregnancy only to twins—rather than to a single fetus—some doctors believe the decision should rest with the mother. If abortion is legal, and she wishes to reduce a pregnancy from triplets to a single baby, what ethical reason is there to object? Medically, the biggest danger of fetal reduction is losing the entire pregnancy, whether it is reduced to twins or to a single fetus.

In reality, couples often find the decision to reduce their pregnancy agonizing. They wanted this pregnancy very much, and to intentionally abort some of the fetuses makes them feel guilty and depressed. One study showed that these feelings, strongest after the selective abortion, also reappeared several months after childbirth, perhaps because once the surviving babies are born, the children lost can be more vividly imagined.[5] Aware of these haunted feelings, members of the Triplet Connection, a group dedicated to supporting families with triplets, has said that couples need to be better informed about raising triplets before they choose to reduce a pregnancy to twins.

A 1995 article in *Woman's Day* describes a Massachusetts nurse who became pregnant with quadruplets after a

GIFT procedure. She finally decided to reduce her pregnancy from quadruplets to triplets. "It was an awful choice," she said in an interview. "Up until the day we walked in there, we weren't sure if we were doing the right thing. That night I cried for the baby I would never hold in my arms."[6] Couples who undergo fetal reduction often speak of the procedure in terms of sacrifice: some of the fetuses must die so that the others may live.

Fetal reduction is quite rare. According to one study, between 1986 and 1991, only 463 were performed at the world's largest centers for the procedure. Still, no one wants to see fetal reduction become a mainstay of modern medicine. Indeed, the twelve authors of the study, obstetricians who saw patients wanting selective abortion, wrote: "It must be stressed that all of the authors of this publication view multifetal pregnancy reduction as a temporary need until such time as better assisted reproductive techniques obviate the necessity for its use."[7]

Preventing Multiple Births

A much better way to limit multiple births, of course, is to prevent them from ever getting started. A better understanding of proper drug dosages, combined with careful monitoring, has helped reduce the number of multiple births caused by fertility drugs like hMG.

In an effort to reduce the number of multiple births that occur during IVF, some groups are investigating ways to limit the number of embryos transferred. If only one or two embryos are transferred, then only a single baby or twins could be born. Remember, however, that transferring several embryos increases the likelihood that even one will grow properly. This is especially true for women older than 40.

In 1996, it appeared as if the ASRM would soon recommend that fertility clinics limit the number of embryos transferred to women under 40 to three or four. The goal of the intended guidelines was to produce no quadruplets and to reduce the rate of triplets from 5 percent to 1 or 2 percent of pregnancies.[8]

These guidelines are recommendations only. Clinics would be free to disregard them. Other countries, however, have written laws expressly stating the permissible number of embryos to be transferred. In the United Kingdom, for example, only three embryos can be transferred, regardless of the age of the woman. Physicians who violate this law can be fined and imprisoned.

While limiting the number of embryos available for transfer solves the problem of multiple births, it adds the problem of too many embryos. Often, more embryos are created than will be transferred. If five or more eggs are placed with sperm in a laboratory dish, five or more eggs may very well be fertilized. Yet only three or four are destined for transfer. What should be done with the surplus embryos? To address this problem, embryologists have developed a way to freeze the surplus embryos.

Freezing Embryos

In March 1984, the world's first baby to spend time as a frozen embryo was born in Australia.[9] Alan Trounson was the embryologist responsible for this new chapter in reproductive technology. By immersing embryos in liquid nitrogen at −385°F (−232°C), scientists could stop cell growth and achieve a sort of suspended animation. They found that about 60 percent of embryos survive thawing. The frozen embryos could remain like this indefinitely. *Cryopreservation* was a technique first developed for use with livestock. Cattle farmers had been using the technique for years with prized cattle embryos they wished to save or ship.

With cryopreservation, it becomes possible for a woman to undergo only one cycle of fertility drugs to produce all the embryos she will ever need. A few of the embryos can be transferred immediately and the remainder frozen. The frozen embryos can be thawed and used the next month if

114

her first cycle of IVF fails. If pregnancy is achieved, the frozen embryos can be thawed several years later, when the couple is ready for another child. The advantage of using frozen embryos is that the woman need not repeat treatment with fertility drugs. With the use of frozen embryos, IVF becomes safer and cheaper.

Cryopreservation gives couples four choices concerning their surplus embryos. They can have their embryos destroyed, make them available to the fertility clinic for research, donate them to another infertile couple, or freeze them with liquid nitrogen for possible future use. Faced with this rather unappealing menu of options, most couples elect to freeze their surplus embryos.

Choosing to freeze the embryos simply pushes back the moment when a final decision must be made. In Britain, a law that went into effect in 1991 states that couples must make a decision regarding their frozen embryos every 5 years. They can either use them in an IVF cycle, donate them, or extend freezing for another 5 years. Unclaimed embryos will be destroyed. In August 1996, over the objections of some pro-life groups, the first batch of embryos affected by the 1991 law—a total of 3,300 embryos—were destroyed.[10]

In the United States, no such legal limit exists. Instead, most clinics have adopted a policy of ending the period of frozen storage the year the woman who contributed the eggs turns 50 years old. Although embryos can be frozen indefinitely, in theory, no country in the world has given its blessing to this kind of extended storage.

The population of frozen embryos in the United States could easily people a town the size of Lincoln, Nebraska. They number in the tens of thousands. These beings are neither living nor dead. They carry all the genetic information needed to build a human being and yet consist only of a few cells themselves. They are 2 or 3 days old, months shy of birth.

All these frozen embryos represent the dreams and

115

hopes of infertile couples. Yet only a few of them are earmarked for thawing and future use. The rest belong to couples who have ended fertility treatment, either because they have created their family or failed to. They have no plans to transfer the embryo into the woman's uterus, but they can't bring themselves to release their embryos from deep storage. The yearly bill for embryo storage—ranging from $150 to $600—arrives, and they pay it. To stop paying for storage and decide an alternative fate for their embryo would require accepting that this embryo will never become their child. This act of acceptance, this final evaporation of hope, can be extremely difficult.

Just as parents must decide who will care for their children in the event of their deaths or divorce, couples electing to freeze embryos must make this decision. Many clinics require couples to sign a document describing the rights of each partner in the event of a separation or divorce.

In 1983, a wealthy American couple died in a plane crash in Chile, leaving behind an estate worth more than $1 million and two frozen embryos at a clinic in Australia. The couple, Mario and Elsa Rios of Los Angeles, had left the clinic no instructions about what to do in this situation. Although it was unlikely that the embryos would thaw properly—cryopreservation was still in its infancy when they were frozen—the tragedy prompted a public debate. Should the embryos be destroyed? Should they be donated to another couple? If they thawed and developed successfully, would the babies be heirs to their parents' estate?

The clinic initially agreed to store the embryos. A few years later, however, it made plans to destroy them. This sparked such an enormous public uproar that in 1987 the clinic reversed its position and discussed giving them to a childless couple. However as late as 1989, the Rios embryos remained in storage.

Divorce, too, can throw the fate of frozen embryos into question, as couples fight for possession and control of their embryos. The outcome of such custody cases depends on whether the judge thinks of the embryo as a living child, an unborn fetus, or something that has human potential but whose destruction may be justified. Different judges have reached vastly different conclusions on this issue. Such contradictory judgments could be seen as judicial chaos. Or they could be viewed as reflections of public disagreement over what, exactly, is the proper moral and legal status of a frozen embryo.

In 1988, Junior and Mary Sue Davis had seven embryos frozen at a Knoxville, Tennessee, clinic. Mary Sue had been unable to get pregnant with IVF. When the couple divorced, a year later, they battled over the fate of their embryos. They had never signed a legally binding consent form regarding the future of the embryos in the event of divorce. Mary Sue wanted the right to become pregnant with them. Junior wanted them destroyed.

In September 1989, a judge ruled that the embryos were "children, in vitro," and awarded them to Mary Sue. Junior bitterly protested the decision. In the face of his objection, Mary Sue said she would donate them to the clinic so that they could be used by another infertile couple. Again, her ex-husband protested and won an appeal.

Eventually, the case made its way to the Tennessee Supreme Court. That court decided that Junior's right not to procreate overrode Mary Sue's right to have a child. (Some observers noted that this was similar to the right of a pregnant woman to have an abortion if she chose regardless of her partner's wishes.) By order of the state Supreme Court, the embryos were released to Junior in June 1993. He retrieved the embryos from the fertility clinic and had them destroyed.

A couple of years later, in New York, the court case of Maureen Kent Kass and her husband, Steven, began in a similar fashion. Maureen and Steven filed for divorce in July 1993, just 2 months after freezing five embryos. They, too, disagreed over the future of their embryos. Maureen wanted them available for future transfer. Steven wanted them made available for infertility research and then destroyed.

In early 1995, a judge awarded Maureen the right to determine the fate of her embryos. This judge reasoned that a man who creates an embryo through sexual intercourse has no right to compel the woman he impregnated to end the pregnancy or to carry it to term. The same principle should hold true, argued the judge, when embryos are created through IVF.

Two different court cases led to two different judgments. These ugly scenarios show how very emotional the issue of frozen embryos can be. These are not living children, and yet the men and women responsible for their creation are acting almost as if they are. Such custody disputes are extremely rare, but that doesn't mean they are unimportant or irrelevant. They offer valuable insight into the moral issues at stake in high-tech fertility medicine.

8

A NEW INDUSTRY NEEDS REGULATION

Helping people have babies—what could be wrong with that? Plenty, according to many reasonable people. Scandal at a high-profile California clinic recently created shocking headlines and triggered demands for criminal penalties for fertility doctors who intentionally mishandle embryos. Laboratory errors elsewhere have resulted in a call for tighter quality control.

Some of these criticisms have led to reforms in the business of laboratory conception. Certainly all of them have helped shape it. The controversy surrounding fertility medicine is hardly surprising. Fertility treatment is, after all, a business enterprise as well as a scientific one. It also happens to be an extremely profitable business. The field manages to combine human reproduction, already a touchy subject, with big egos, enormous desperation, and large amounts of money.

Couples struggling with fertility, not surprisingly, often disagree with these critiques. They don't want to hear from the priest who condemns their last chance at having a baby of their own flesh and blood. They don't want to believe that the clinic where they spent thousands of dollars was hyping its success rates. Women don't want to see themselves as pawns pushed toward motherhood by enormous social pressures. They believe that no one who has not walked in their shoes can feel their pain and fully understand the choices they have made. Theirs is a roulette game that others, who have already won the big prize, might watch but can never play.

The 1980s saw assisted reproductive technology grow from a medical novelty into a well-established business. Like other businesses, the fertility industry began to vie for customers with advertisements, glossy brochures, and patient-education seminars. Consumer advocates and government watchdogs observed this competition uneasily. At times, the fertility industry seemed to have more in common with the sales of sneakers than the practice of medicine. The observers had no objection to assisted reproductive technology itself but rather to the way it was being marketed to the American public.

The desperation of infertile couples left them vulnerable to clinics' claims. Ordinarily careful consumers, they found it very difficult to gather the information they needed to evaluate the expertise and success rate of a particular fertility clinic. They found it impossible to verify advertised success rates. No Better Business Bureau of fertility clinics existed. To someone without a background in medicine, the finer points of fertility medicine were incomprehensible. In some cases, infertile couples were easily swayed by fertility clinic advertisements featuring portraits of babies designed to tug at their heartstrings. Even as the odds of bringing home a baby were very low, the costs were very high: at that time, one in vitro fertilization cycle cost about $8,000. Most of this money came out of their own pockets since few health insurance policies covered infertility treatment.

The potential exploitation of vulnerable couples worsened when IVF was no longer the province of a few, highly experienced specialists. In 1985, there were only thirty or so clinics in the United States offering IVF. The people who pioneered IVF in this country—men and women like Drs. Howard and Georgeanna Jones at the Jones Institute for Reproductive Medicine in Norfolk, Virginia—had worked hard to gain the public trust. But by the late 1980s, the number of facilities offering IVF had increased six-fold. (By 1994, there were more than 300 clinics.)

Unfortunately, not every clinic that offered IVF had the experience of the Jones Institute, to say the least. Laboratory conception services varied widely in size and experience. Some fertility clinics were part of the most prestigious university medical centers. Others were quite small. A few clinics served hundreds of couples each year and some clinics saw less than a dozen. Some doctors had extensive backgrounds in reproductive medicine and had apprenticed at the Jones Institute or in England or Australia. Other doctors had learned in vitro techniques in a few weekend seminars.

Competition among the clinics increased drastically. Infertile couples were spending $30 million to $40 million a year on infertility treatment and many hospitals, eager to share in this new source of wealth, were racing to sign up physicians and embryologists willing to offer IVF. In the scramble to gain a foothold in the highly lucrative business of making babies, clinics boasted of high success rates. Their ads, designed to appeal to the emotions of eager patients, left out such niceties as their experience and track record. It was a volatile mix: desperate patients, procedures whose effectiveness was difficult to gauge, and doctors whose past successes made them feel like gods.

Success rates among IVF clinics varied widely. This was due, in part, to variations among patients. But success ultimately depended, to a great extent, on the expertise of the people who conducted the procedures. One physician might be better at retrieving eggs or transferring embryos than another. An embryologist in one clinic might be better at evaluating eggs and coaxing embryos to grow than another. In this field, experience mattered—a lot. No one, no matter how talented, could become proficient at IVF until he or she practiced on a large number of patients.

New clinics, with less experienced physicians and embryologists, were understandably reluctant to disclose that they had few babies to show for their efforts. They often calculated their success rates differently than more established clinics. To get a higher, better, success rate, a clinic might count pregnancies achieved rather than babies born, thus disregarding the substantial miscarriage rate. Or it might count biochemical pregnancies rather than clinical pregnancies, ignoring miscarriages that occurred even before ultrasound could verify the pregnancy. Some clinics based their figures solely on women who underwent egg retrieval, thereby leaving out all the women who underwent ovarian stimulation but whose ovaries didn't produce eggs that could be transferred. Other clinics improved their statistics by counting only their easiest cases, leaving out couples that included women older than 35, perhaps, or men with impaired fertility.

The Government Gets Involved

In some cases, the claims of fertility clinics sounded too good to be true. Indeed, upon further investigation, they weren't true. By the late 1980s, consumer complaints had attracted the attention of the U.S. government and several government agencies took a long, hard look at the booming fertility business.

What they found was disturbing. In 1988, the Office of Technology Assessment (OTA) published a report on scientific, legal, and ethical issues surrounding infertility.[1] In it,

122

the OTA noted that many clinics were signing up patients without telling the patients that the clinics had never had a live birth. The Federal Trade Commission (FTC), acting in its role to prevent misleading advertising, began investigating exaggerated success rates and deceptive advertising. The most significant changes in the industry, however, came as a result of hearings held by a congressional subcommittee on business regulation chaired by Representative Ron Wyden, a Democrat from Oregon.

Speaking at a hearing held in 1989, Wyden observed that infertile couples were "vulnerable to exploitation and to those who would unfairly try to rip them off." He declared that, "American families are entitled to the facts. They ought to be protected from the hype about the fertility business." He vowed that his subcommittee would thoroughly investigate the fertility industry.[2]

In 1991, the FTC won five cease-and-desist cases against fertility clinics in Arizona, California, Colorado, and New York. In at least one case, these investigations resulted in a lawsuit against a fertility clinic by former patients.

After an investigation by the New York City Department of Consumer Affairs, Mt. Sinai Medical Center paid $4 million to settle a lawsuit filed by hundreds of former infertility patients. The clinic had published misleading success rates in its brochure.[3]

Wyden's hearings led to the development of two new tools with which infertile couples could evaluate the claims of clinics. First, the subcommittee developed a guide to IVF clinics for consumers. For the first time, information on each clinic—number of births, types of fertility problems handled, qualifications of lab personnel, and ages of patients treated—was available to everyone.

Second, Wyden introduced legislation that would require clinics to report their pregnancy success rates to the secretary of the Department of Health and Human Services. If they didn't, they would be fined $10,000. The law, known as the Fertility Clinic Success Rate and Certification Act, went into effect in 1992.

When the government investigated the fertility business, it found that the laboratories used for high-tech procedures were not monitored by any independent agency. One of the provisions of the Fertility Clinic Success Rate and Certification Act of 1992 was to create a model program for the certification of embryo laboratories. The law is expected to improve the quality of embryo labs.

Unfortunately, even the best-organized lab cannot prevent human error or, more disturbingly, intentional wrongdoing. Human error has played a role in airplane crashes, surgical mistakes, and maternity floor mix-ups. The fertility industry has been around long enough to have seen the consequences of human error in its laboratories too. However awful the consequences of human error in other settings, mistakes in the embryo lab seem to have an added dimension of freakishness and suffering.

In 1995, a Dutch couple, using the pseudonyms Wilma and Willem Stuart, went to the press with the story of a laboratory mistake. In late 1993, Wilma had given birth to twin sons, Teun and Koen, who had been conceived through IVF at a clinic in Utrecht. But after only a few months Koen looked noticeably different from the rest of his family. He had darker skin than his brother and fuzzy hair. These differences were so obvious that he attracted questions and stares from neighbors in the Stuart's quiet Dutch town.

Finally, the Stuarts sought DNA testing. The tests showed that Koen's father was not Willem. A further examination of records at the fertility clinic revealed that a man from Aruba, a Caribbean island, had been in the clinic with his wife on the same day as the Stuarts. A technician accidentally reused a pipette that contained sperm from this man during the Stuart's IVF procedure.

Although the couple felt very strongly that the clinic— and the public—should know of the error, they never considered abandoning Koen. In an interview with *Jet* magazine, Willem said, "To give him up has never even occurred to me. You cannot give a child up like garbage . . . We are so happy he is there, we would never consider giving him up. He is our child."[4]

And the man in Aruba? According to *Newsweek*, his first words upon learning that he had a son living with a Dutch couple were, "Do they love the child?"[5]

Even more shocking than laboratory mistakes are allegations of deliberate wrongdoing. Consider the story of the Center for Reproductive Health at the University of California, Irvine. In June 1995, university investigators shut down the clinic after publicly alleging that three doctors there, in some fifty cases, took eggs or embryos without permission and gave them to other patients. The investigators claimed that this resulted in the birth of at least seven children. The three accused physicians were Jose Balmaceda, Sergio Stone, and clinic director Ricardo H. Asch, the doctor who pioneered the GIFT procedure.

Debbie and John Challender, of Corona, California, were among the many couples who sought treatment from Asch. In 1991, already the parents of an adopted boy, they prepared for a GIFT procedure. Debbie produced forty-six eggs, twenty-one of which fertilized. Sick from the fertility drugs used to stimulate such a large number of eggs, Debbie elected to wait a few months before transferring the embryos. She and John requested that the twenty-one embryos be frozen. Two months later, she underwent embryo transfer and a baby boy was born on August 24, 1992.

In May 1995, a team of newspaper reporters from the *Orange County Register* presented the Challenders with their medical records. The newspaper had been given the records by three administrators from the clinic who suspected wrongdoing but had been unable to convince the university to pursue their concerns. Debbie and John learned, for the first time, that only eighteen of the twenty-one embryos had ever been frozen. Three embryos had been transferred into another clinic patient the same day the other embryos were frozen. To their horror, Debbie and John discovered that twins, a boy and a girl, had been born to another couple.

The Challenders hired a lawyer. Although they wanted to know whether the twins were happy and loved, they had no desire to wrest the children from the only home the children had ever known. Adoptive parents themselves, they understood that being a mother and father was more than contributing an egg and a sperm.

In the meantime, state and federal authorities began investigating the claims of patients and former clinic employees. For his part, Asch denied making improper embryo transfers in an ABC-TV interview in late 1995. Facing civil suits from former patients, he sold his two California homes and moved to Mexico City. In November 1996, he was indicted by a federal grand jury on thirty-five counts of mail fraud. A new state law makes the theft of human eggs a crime.

As the government scrutinized clinics, fertility specialists took a long, hard look at themselves. "Unfortunately, this industry has developed with only a few of the safeguards in place that are required to create honest market conditions," wrote Norbert Gleicher, editor of the *Journal of Assisted Reproduction and Genetics*, in 1995. "How can we sell a product if we do not know how good it is? How can we expect the public to continue to buy it without complaints if we cannot tell them what we are selling?"[6]

Fertility doctors realized that if they didn't establish voluntary guidelines for themselves, the government would do it for them. They were eager to avoid the plight of their British counterparts, whose actions are governed, in part, by legislation. It is the law, for instance, rather than profession-al guidelines that forbids a British doctor from transferring more than three embryos into a woman.

Looking Toward the Future

It's easy to forget just how new assisted reproductive technology is. The phrase "test-tube baby" seems like it's been part of the English language forever and most people could probably give an elementary description of in vitro fertilization. The field *is* still quite new, however. Many of its early pioneers continue to be actively engaged in research and clinical practice. Although Steptoe died in 1988, Edwards remains at Bourn Hall, the fertility clinic he and Steptoe started outside Cambridge. Howard and Georgeanna Jones, both in their 80s, are still with the clinic that bears their name. The innovative work of Alan Trounson continues to make news periodically.

Critics have focused on the long-term effects of treatment, particularly the possible link between fertility drugs and cancer. They question not only the safety and efficacy of new procedures, but also the use of proven procedures in new ways. There is wide agreement, for instance, that IVF is an appropriate treatment for women with blocked or missing fallopian tubes. But is it appropriate to recommend it to couples with male infertility? Or unexplained fertility? No studies support the benefits of IVF over other forms of treatment.

The enthusiasm that infertile couples have for new treatments can, in some cases, make it more difficult for medical scientists to design careful studies to compare a new treatment against an older treatment. Couples eager to try a new procedure are often unwilling to enter a clinical trial that examines the efficacy of the procedure because only half of the patients receive the new, experimental treatment. The rest must receive the older, proven treatment. Infertile couples don't want to risk being put in the group that doesn't receive it. They may also feel that they don't have time to waste in scientific studies. The result is a kind of Catch-22 situation: no one wants to take the time and energy testing a new procedure because they are already convinced it works.

There is another reason that fertility research is difficult to conduct in the United States—scientists who work on fertilized eggs and embryos can't get federal funding. Although the government has created ethical guidelines that permit embryo research in some instances, the strong anti-abortion lobby has effectively blocked the government from ever funding such experiments. Since funding carries with it a certain degree of regulative power, the lack of federal funding means that fertility scientists are not influenced by federally established research guidelines and standards. Some infertility research involving embryos does take place in the United States, but it is all conducted with private funds.

Finally, fertility research has not been taken up as a consumer cause. People affected by many medical conditions, including AIDS and breast cancer have pulled together and lobbied for more research money. This has not been the case with infertility and the people it touches, perhaps because of the wide variety of causes and conditions that fall under the umbrella label of "infertility."

9

THE
END
OF
FERTILITY
TREATMENT

Unfortunately, about 35 percent of couples who undergo conventional forms of treatment for infertility will ultimately end up disappointed. The odds are much worse for couples who decide to try in vitro fertilization—about 80 percent of these couples see their dreams go unrealized. A couple who attempts four or five cycles of IVF is more likely to succeed than a couple who attempts only one or two, but even so, the odds are against them.

Despite repeated failures and enormous expense, some couples find it extremely difficult to stop treatment. They feel courageous continuing against the odds and fear a sense of failure when they consider stopping. The support group RESOLVE helps couples set goals and limits on medical treatment. If a couple decides to stop medical treatment, RESOLVE can also provide information and support regarding adoption and living without children.

Seeking to Adopt

Most people with impaired fertility investigate medical treatment before looking into adoption. Despite advice given by well-meaning friends and family, adoption is not a cure for infertility. It is a cure for the desire to parent. For some people, having a genetic connection to their children is tremendously important. While undergoing IVF, a woman who lost 120 members of her family in the Holocaust told *The New York Times*: "I wanted my child to be a biological Jew . . . I did not want to be the period in the sentence."[1]

Other people are daunted by the uncertainty of the adoption process. After years of failed medical treatments and thousands of dollars spent with no result, they may feel unable, emotionally, to handle the risk of a birth mother changing her mind. Moving from treatment to adoption may feel like substituting one type of anxiety for another. The high costs involved in adopting a healthy infant may also be daunting.

For many people, however, their desire for a genetic connection to the future is less strong than their desire to become a mother or father to a child. Once they begin exploring adoption, they learn that loving a child depends not on some magical bonding that takes place at delivery but upon a willingness to love.

People choosing adoption are faced with several options. They can work through an agency—an office that works to match birth parents and adoptive parents, offers legal services, and may even have psychological counselors. Or the couple may elect to handle those issues themselves and adopt independently with the help of an attorney. (Five states in the United States have banned private adoption.)

The couple may try to adopt a child born in the United States or they may contact an agency that arranges international adoptions of children from Asia, India, eastern Europe, or South America. They also must decide whether they're more comfortable with a closed adoption, in which no identifying details about the birth parents are released, or whether they'd prefer to know the birth parents.

Although many adoptive parents start the process imagining themselves with a healthy newborn baby of their own ethnic background, many soon find themselves open to adopting a child who doesn't fit that picture. They may consider a toddler or young child to adopt. They may find they have something to offer a child with special physical or mental needs. Many parents adopt children of a different race, after carefully thinking about how they will raise the child so as to honor his or her ethnic heritage.

For parents who wish to adopt a healthy, white newborn baby in the United States, the wait can be 5 years or more. This wasn't the case several decades ago. Adoption is different today than it once was. One reason is that in the past, single women felt enormous societal pressure to give up their babies for adoption. Today, more and more single women are raising their babies. In addition, abortion is now available throughout the United States; a 1973 Supreme Court decision made it legal in every state.

Young women with an ill-timed pregnancy have more choices than ever before, including participation in an open or closed adoption. Pregnant teenagers are more likely than women in their 20s to choose adoption over single motherhood. Creating an adoption plan for a baby can be a loving and responsible choice. Some adoption agencies allow the birth mother to select the couple that will adopt the baby. Open adoption allows the birth mother to receive news about the baby and to feel assured that the baby is well cared for and happy.

Choosing a Life Without Children

Living without children—sometimes called childfree living—is one option for infertile couples who believe that they can build a rewarding life around their marriage, career, or hobby. They recognize that a childfree lifestyle has unique opportunities for education, travel, and leisure. If they wish to engage in nurturing children or young people, they can volunteer with Scout groups or the Big Brother/Big Sister program or become involved in the lives of nieces and nephews. Deliberately choosing this lifestyle changes their definition of themselves: they are no longer infertile but rather childfree.

Living childfree is different from drifting into a lifestyle better described as "childless." Childfree living is an active choice, not a failure to act. The choice may occur gradually. A couple starts by taking time off from medical treatment and then, as the months stretch into years, they realize that they have made a decision not to adopt or to undergo further medical treatment. At that point they may decide to think of themselves as childfree.

Helen and Dave Krouse decided to live childfree after 6 years of medical treatment failed to make them parents. They considered adoption but decided that after the crushing disappointment of repeated miscarriages, they could not face the emotional risks involved in adoption. Helen explains their feelings like this:

> When making that decision, you've got to look at what you have. Are you willing to go on any more roller coasters? We weren't. We were tired of not knowing what was going to happen next week or next month and getting our hopes built up. I think in our heart of hearts we believed that if I had never miscarried, we might have had the emotional energy it takes to proceed with adoption.

Their love for each other was another important part of their decision to stop their efforts to become parents and to live childfree. Helen says:

> We looked at the situation and decided we still had each other. In our minds, the worst thing that could

happen to us was not that we would fail at becoming parents, but that we would lose each other as a result of infertility or treatment, that the stress of pursuing the pregnancies would drive us apart.

We are more in love now than we were then. Infertility, in a lot of ways, helped our relationship. It increased our communication skills. It taught us to accept the other person's point-of-view unconditionally and to go with it. Like when I wanted to do treatment, and he didn't, and he agreed to it anyway. He had to be the one to give me the shots so it's not like he can decide just not to participate. We basically just learned a lot about each other, and about ourselves, and we're better for it.

Medicine has made great strides in recent decades to make parenthood a reality for couples struggling with infertility. There is a wealth of information and support available for people who want a baby. Still, much remains to be learned about the causes of and cures for infertility. Many couples who turn to medical science for help will meet with crushing disappointment. But some couples—more today, in fact, than ever before—will find a miracle.

GLOSSARY

abstinence—choosing not to engage in some activity, especially sexual intercourse.

amniocentesis—a medical test that involves inserting a needle into the uterus and removing a small amount of amniotic fluid. This fluid contains old fetal cells, which can be tested to determine whether the developing child has any one of a number of chromosomal defects.

amniotic fluid—the liquid that surrounds a developing fetus.

antisperm antibodies—antibodies that attach to the sperm and prevent them from making their journey to the egg.

assisted hatching—a micromanipulation technique that involves drilling a tiny hole in the outer layer of the embryo to encourage implantation.

assisted insemination—the placement of sperm directly into the woman's vagina, cervix, or uterus by a physician with a plastic tube or syringe. The sperm may come from the woman's partner or it may come from an anonymous donor.

assisted reproductive technology—the name for several laboratory procedures that involve removing eggs from the ovaries and either combining them with sperm in a laboratory dish or transferring them with sperm back into the body. See entries for *in vitro fertilization, gamete intrafallopian transfer*, and *zygote intrafallopian transfer*.

balloon tuboplasty—a medical procedure in which a tiny balloon is inserted into a fallopian tube. When the balloon is inflated, the material responsible for the tube's blockage may be displaced, allowing eggs to travel through the tube to the uterus.

basal body temperature—the temperature of the body upon waking in the morning before any activity. By charting her basal body temperature, a woman can pinpoint when ovulation occurs.

cervical mucus incompatibility—during ovulation, instead of becoming thin and less acidic, the cervical mucus remains inhospitable to sperm.

cervix—the lower end of the uterus that extends into the vagina. Sperm must enter the cervix and pass through the uterus to reach the fallopian tubes.

cesarean-section—a medical procedure in which babies are delivered through a surgical incision in the abdomen.

chlamydia—a sexually transmitted disease caused by a bacterial infection.

clinical pregnancy—a pregnancy that has been confirmed by viewing the fetus with ultrasound at 5 to 8 weeks after fertilization.

clomiphene—a drug that induces ovulation by stimulating the pituitary gland. Sold under the brand name Clomid or Serophene.

conjoined—joined together. Conjoined twins are attached and share some organs.

cryopreservation—a technique for freezing embryos conceived in the laboratory for future thawing and transfer to the uterus. The embryos are immersed in liquid nitrogen and cooled to a temperature of –385°F (–231°C). Cell growth stops and starts again only when the embryos are properly thawed.

diethylstilbestrol (DES)—a synthetic hormone prescribed to prevent miscarriage in pregnant women between 1940 and 1971. The daughters of women who took DES are at risk for uterine abnormalities and vaginal and cervical cancer.

donor egg—eggs taken from the ovaries of a fertile woman and donated to an infertile woman and her partner for in vitro fertilization and embryo transfer.

donor sperm—sperm used for assisted insemination that comes from a man other than the woman's partner. Donor sperm is available, by prescription, from commercial sperm banks.

ectopic pregnancy—instead of growing in the uterus, the fertilized egg grows in the fallopian tube. If left untreated, ectopic pregnancy can be life-threatening because the tube will rupture and cause internal bleeding.

egg—the female reproductive cell.

egg retrieval—removing mature eggs from the ovaries during the in vitro fertilization process.

ejaculate—to release semen through the penis.

embryo—term used to describe the fertilized egg as it divides and grows during the first eight weeks of pregnancy. After this point, the embryo is usually referred to as a fetus.

embryo transfer—embryos created during in vitro fertilization are placed in the woman's uterus via a thin plastic tube.

endocrine disruptors—human-made chemicals that mimic natural hormones.

endometrial biopsy—scraping a small sample of the tissue from the lining of the uterus after ovulation to see whether it is capable of nurturing a fertilized egg.

endometriosis—a poorly understood disease in which tissue from the lining of the uterus grows on the ovaries and other pelvic organs.

endometrium—the lining of the uterus.

erection—the stiffening of the penis due to a sudden inflow of blood caused by sexual arousal.

estradiol—a type of estrogen. By measuring the level of this hormone in a woman's blood, doctors can determine how quickly her eggs are maturing.

estrogen—this hormone—and another, progesterone—signals the uterine lining to thicken with blood and nutrients in preparation for the arrival of a fertilized egg.

fallopian tube—one of a pair of hollow tubes that extend from either side of the uterus toward the ovaries. The egg travels from the ovary to the uterus through the fallopian tube. Fertilization usually occurs in the fallopian tubes.

fertility drugs—drugs that stimulate the ovaries to produce eggs. Clomiphene and hMG are two frequently prescribed fertility drugs.

fertilization—the act of the sperm penetrating the egg and the combining of their genetic material to create an embryo.

fertilized egg—the egg immediately after fertilization, before it has started to divide.

fetal reduction— aborting some, but not all, fetuses in a multiple pregnancy. Fetal reduction, also called selective abortion, is used to reduce a pregnancy of four or more fetuses to twins or triplets.

fetus—term used to describe the developing embryo after the first eight weeks of growth during pregnancy and up until birth.

follicle—a sac in the ovary that contains the developing egg.

follicle-stimulating hormone—the hormone that stimulates the egg to mature inside its follicle.

gamete—gamete is a scientific term for eggs and sperm.

gamete intrafallopian transfer (GIFT)—eggs are removed from the woman and sperm is collected from the man. The eggs and sperm are deposited together in an unblocked fallopian tube. Unlike in vitro fertilization, conception occurs inside the body rather than in the laboratory.

gestational surrogate mother—see entries for *host uterus* and *surrogate mother*.

gonorrhea—a sexually transmitted disease caused by a bacterial infection. It is also called the clap.

host uterus—a procedure in which one woman carries the embryo produced by the egg of another woman. After an egg and sperm are taken from a man and woman for in vitro fertilization, the embryo is transferred into the uterus of another woman. The woman with the host uterus will carry the pregnancy and relinquish the baby at birth to the couple. See also *surrogate mother*.

human chorionic gonadotropin (hCG)—when given as a drug, this hormone triggers ovulation by readying the mature eggs for release from the follicles. It is known by the brand name Profasi.

human menopausal gonadotropin (hMG)—a combination of follicle-stimulating hormone and luteinizing hormone that is given as a drug and sold under the brand name Pergonal or Humegon.

hyperstimulation—a condition that occurs when ovaries swell too large and excess fluid collects in the abdominal cavity. The use of fertility drugs must be carefully monitored to prevent hyperstimulation.

hysterosalpingogram (HSG)—a special X ray of the uterus and fallopian tubes taken after dye is injected into the uterus via the cervix. By examining the path of the dye through the uterus and tubes, the physician can determine if there are any blockages.

implantation—attachment of the egg to the uterine lining. Implantation occurs about 14 days after fertilization.

infertility—the inability to achieve pregnancy after one year of regular sexual intercourse without birth control. Either the woman, the man, or both may have fertility problems. Also recurrent miscarriage that results in the inability to stay pregnant.

intracytoplasmic sperm injection (ICSI)—in the laboratory, a single sperm is injected directly into the egg.

intrauterine device (IUD)—a birth-control method. It is inserted into the uterus and prevents a fertilized egg from implanting and developing properly.

intrauterine insemination—the placement of sperm directly into the uterus by a physician with a plastic tube or syringe.

in vitro fertilization (IVF)—conception outside of the body. One or more eggs are removed from the woman and combined with sperm from the man in a laboratory dish. The resulting embryo is transferred to the woman's uterus about 48 hours later.

laparoscopy—a medical procedure in which a special tube with its own light source can be used to look directly at the internal organs.

luteinizing hormone—the hormone that prompts the follicle to release the egg.

male impotence—a condition in which a man has a healthy reproductive system and is producing normal sperm, but is unable to maintain an erection during sexual intercourse. As a result, he cannot transfer his sperm to a woman's vagina.

menopause—the absence of ovulation and menstruation. Menopause normally occurs when a woman is in her late 40s or early 50s. When menopause occurs in young women in their 20s or 30s, it is known as premature menopause.

menstrual period—the portion of a woman's menstrual cycle in which she discharges blood and material that has built up along the uterine walls in preparation for possible implantation of a fertilized egg. Her period is a signal that there is no fertilized egg. In other words, she is not pregnant.

micromanipulation—laboratory techniques performed on eggs or sperm or fertilized eggs to improve the success rate of in vitro fertilization.

microsurgery—see *micromanipulation*.

miscarriage—the end of pregnancy due to the death of an

embryo or early fetus. The woman may experience bleeding from the vagina and cramps, as with a menstrual period. Tissue from the fetus may be expelled with the bleeding.

monitoring—frequent, even daily, visits to the fertility clinic for ultrasound examination and a blood test to determine whether a woman's ovaries are in danger of being overstimulated by fertility drugs.

monogamous—having sexual intercourse with only one partner over a period of time. You have sex with only one partner who has sex with only you.

multiple birth—the birth of more than one baby. Most multiple births are twins.

ovary—one of the two female sex glands located on each side of the uterus very near the top of the fallopian tubes. The ovaries produce eggs and hormones.

ovulation—the release of the mature egg from its follicle in the ovary. This is the time of the month when a woman is fertile.

palpation—to examine by touching.

pelvic inflammatory disease—an infection in the uterus, fallopian tubes, and pelvis, often caused by a sexually transmitted disease. Scar tissue from pelvic inflammatory disease can block the tubes.

pituitary gland—a small oval organ attached to the brain that releases a variety of hormones.

polycystic ovarian disease—a disease in which the ovaries fail to ovulate and produce tiny cysts instead.

postcoital test—a sample of cervical mucus is taken several hours after a woman has sexual intercourse. The postcoital test is used to see how well the sperm can swim in the cervical mucus just before ovulation.

preimplantation genetic diagnosis—a medical procedure in which a single cell is removed from a very young embryo that has been conceived in the laboratory. The cell is tested for chromosomal defects. If defects are found, the embryo is discarded.

progesterone—this hormone and another, estrogen, signal

140

the uterine lining to thicken with blood and nutrients in preparation for the arrival of a fertilized egg.

prostate gland—an organ at the base of the urethra in males. It secretes a fluid that mixes with sperm to form semen.

scrotum—the bag of skin that holds the testicles.

secondary infertility—the inability to conceive again by a couple who has one biological child already.

semen—the mix of sperm (2 percent) and fluids (98 percent) that is released during ejaculation.

septum—a membrane that divides an organ or tissue into two halves.

sexually transmitted disease (STD)—any infection transmitted through sexual contact, including chlamydia, gonorrhea, and AIDS.

Sims-Hühner test—see *postcoital test*.

singleton—a birth in which one child is delivered.

sperm—the male reproductive cell.

sperm duct—one of a pair of tubes through which sperm and semen travel before ejaculation.

subzonal sperm insertion (SUZI)—a micromanipulation technique in which a single sperm is inserted into the area between the egg and its outer layer, known as the zona.

surrogate mother—a woman who carries a pregnancy for another couple. She relinquishes the baby to the couple at birth. There are two types of surrogates. A woman who is inseminated by the man's sperm is known as a traditional or genetic surrogate. She provides both the egg and the uterus to the pregnancy and is genetically related to the baby. A woman who receives embryos created in the laboratory by the couple is known as a host uterus or gestational surrogate. She provides only a uterus to the pregnancy and lacks any genetic connection to the baby.

testicle—the two male sex glands that hang outside the body in the scrotum. The testicles produce sperm and hormones.

testicular biopsy—a medical procedure in which a small

piece of a testicular tissue is removed. The sample is tested to determine if sperm production is normal.

thyroid gland—a large bilobed gland located at the base of the neck. It produces and releases a number of hormones.

toxemia—a rare disease of pregnancy.

traditional surrogate—see *surrogate mother.*

ultrasound—a device that uses sound waves to take a picture of internal organs.

unexplained infertility—the diagnosis made when no specific reason can be found to explain why a couple is having trouble conceiving.

urethra—a tube that carries urine from the bladder to the outside of the body. In males, this tube also transports semen.

uterus—the hollow organ where the embryo implants and grows during pregnancy.

vagina—the canal that leads to the cervix.

varicocele—a varicose vein in the testicle that can cause an increase in temperature in the testicle. Some physicians believe that this temperature increase results in a reduction in sperm production.

vasectomy—a medical procedure in which the sperm ducts are surgically cut to prevent sperm from leaving the testicles during ejaculation. A means of birth control that intentionally leaves a man infertile.

zona pellucida—the outer layer, or shell, of an egg.

zygote—another name for a fertilized egg.

zygote intrafallopian transfer (ZIFT)—one or more eggs are removed from the woman and combined with sperm from the man in a laboratory dish. Unlike in vitro fertilization, the fertilized eggs—known as zygotes—are transferred to an unblocked fallopian tube rather than to the uterus.

SOURCE
NOTES

Chapter One

The information on the prevalence of infertility in general and specific conditions (like tubal blockage) in particular is drawn from American Society for Reproductive Medicine fact sheets, RESOLVE fact sheets, and patient booklets printed by Serono, a company that manufactures fertility drugs. See especially Serono's "Pathways to Parenthood."

The interview with Helen Krouse was conducted on July 8, 1996.

1. "U.S.'s Rate of Sexual Diseases Is Highest in Developed World." *The New York Times.* November 20, 1996, C21.

2. Carlsen, E. et. al. "Evidence for decreasing quality of semen during past 50 years," *BMJ.* September 12, 1992, 609–613.

   See also Auger, J. et. al. "Decline in semen quality among fertile men in Paris during past 20 years." *New*

England Journal of Medicine. February 2, 1995, 281–285.

For more information on endocrine disruptors, see Colborn, Theo, Dianne Dumanoski, and John Peterson Myers. *Our Stolen Future.* New York: Dutton, 1996.

3. "If You are Contemplating Adoption . . ." *Consumer Reports.* February 1996, p. 55.

Chapter Three

The interviews with Lisa and John Veerlos and Carole and Paul White were conducted on December 6, 1996.

1. Jones, H. and J. Toner. "The Infertile Couple." *New England Journal of Medicine.* December 2, 1993, 1710–1715.

2. Wilcox L. and W. Mosher. "Use of Infertility Services in the United States." *Obstetrics and Gynecology.* July 1993, 122–127.

3. Consumer protection issues involving in vitro fertilization clinics: hearing before the Subcommittee on Regulation, Business Opportunities, and Energy of the Committee on Small Business, House of Representatives, March 9, 1989. JoBeth Williams's testimony appears on pages 122–123 in the official transcript.

Chapter Four

The biographical information for Patrick Steptoe and Robert Edwards comes from "Edwards and Steptoe." *The Biographical Dictionary of Scientists.* Edited by Roy Porter. New York: Oxford University Press, 1994, p. 203 and "Patrick Steptoe." *Current Biography.* Edited by Charles Moritz. New York: HW Wilson Company, 1979.

The biographical information for Lesley and Gilbert John Brown comes from their book *Our Miracle Called Louise: A Parents' Story*. New York: Paddington Press, distributed by Grossett and Dunlap, 1979.

1. "Frenzy in the British Press." *Time*. July 31, 1978, p. 70.

2. *Our Miracle Named Louise: A Parents' Story*. prologue.

3. "Test-Tube Baby: It's a Girl." *Time*. August 8, 1978, p 68.

4. *Our Miracle Named Louise: A Parents' Story*. p. 106.

5. "This is What You Thought About . . .Test-Tube Babies." *Glamour*. June 1982, p. 29.

6. Dawood, M. "In vitro fertilization, gamete intrafallopian transfer, and superovulation with intrauterine insemination: efficacy and potential health hazards on babies delivered." *American Journal of Obstetrics & Gynecology*. April 1996, 1208–1217.

   Friedler, S. "Births in Israel resulting from in-vitro fertilization/embryo transfer, 1982–1989: National Registry of the Israeli Association for Fertility Research," *Human Reproduction*. September 1992, 1159–1163.

7. Golombok, S. et. al. "Families created by the new reproductive technologies: quality of parenting and social and emotional development of the children." *Child Development*. April 1995, 258–298.

   Weaver, S. et. al. "A follow-up study of 'successful' IVF/GIFT couples: social-emotional well-being and adjustment to parenthood," *Journal of Psychosomatic Obstetrics and Gynecology*. 1993, Supplement 14, 5–16.

8. Lawson, Carol. "Celebrated Birth Aside, Teen-Ager is Typical Now." *The New York Times*. October 4, 1993, A18.

Chapter Five

Statistics on success at each stage of IVF process are taken from "Assisted reproductive technology in the United States and Canada: 1994 results generated from the American Society for Reproductive Medicine/Society for Assisted Reproductive Technology Registry," *Fertility and Sterility.* November 1996, p. 697–705.

1. Gabriel, Trip. "High-Tech Pregnancies Test Hope's Limit." *The New York Times.* January 7, 1996, p. 18, for comparison with France.

   "Fertility Clinics: What are the odds?" *Consumer Reports.* February 1996, p. 54, for comparison with Massachusetts.

2. Canadian Royal Commission on New Reproductive Technologies. *Proceed With Care.* Ottawa: Canada Communications Group, 1993. This report on page 526 states that IVF is effective only for blocked tubes. It states that IVF is ineffective for other forms of infertility on pages 518–519.

3. Rossing, M. et. al. "Ovarian tumors in a cohort of infertile women." *New England Journal of Medicine.* September 22, 1994, 771–776.

4. Alikani, M. et. al. "Monozygotic twinning in the human is associated with the zona pellcida architecture," *Human Reproduction.* July 1994, 1318–1321.

5. Skupski, D. et al. "Early diagnosis of conjoined twins in triplet pregnancy after in vitro fertilization and assisted hatching." *Journal of Ultrasound in Medicine.* August 1995, 611.

6. Thompson, Larry. "Fertility with Less Fuss." *Time.* November 14, 1994, p. 79.

7. Handyside, A. et. al. "Pregancies from biopsied human

preimplantation embryos sexed by Y-specific DNA amplification" *Nature*. April 19, 1990, p. 768.

Chapter Six

1. Schmeck, Harold M. Jr. "Birth is Reported in New Technique," *The New York Times*. January 13, 1984, p. 10.

2. "Surrogate Has Baby Conceived in Laboratory." *The New York Times*. April 17, 1986, A26.

3. Organization of Parents Through Surrogacy world wide web site. See http://www.fertilitext.org/surrogacy.html

4. The American Fertility Society. "Guidelines for gamete donation." *Fertility and Sterility*. February 1993, Supplement 1, 6S.

5. Kolata, Gina. "Reproductive Revolution." *The New York Times*. January 11, 1994, A1.

6. Information on the Calvert case came from Liptak, Karen. *Adoption Controversies*. New York: Franklin Watts, 1993, and Kasindorf, Martin. "And Baby Makes Four." *Los Angeles Times Magazine*. January 20, 1991.

7. Check, J.H. et. al., "Successful delivery after age 50: a report of two cases as a result of oocyte donation," *Obstetrics & Gynecology*. May 1993, 835–836.

   Sauer, M. et. al., "Pregnancy after age 50: application of oocyte donation to women after natural menopause." *The Lancet*. February 6, 1993, 321.

   These two medical studies were the first to report birth in post-menopausal women after the use of egg donation.

Chapter Seven

1. Callahan, T., et. al. "The economic impact of multiple-gestation pregnancies and their contribution of assisted-reproduction techniques to their incidence," *New England Journal of Medicine*. July 28, 1994, 244–249.

2. Garel M et al., "Assessment at 1 year of the psychological consequences of having triplets." *Human Reproduction*. May 1992, 729–732.

3. Martin, Antoinette. "Is Society Really Ready for More Multiples?" *The New York Times*. February 8, 1996, B1.

4. Multiple news stories about the Frustaci case ran in 1985. A news story describing the settlement of the lawsuit appeared in *Los Angeles Times*. July 19, 1990, J1.

5. Garel, M. et. al. "Psychological effects of embryonal reduction. From the decision making to four months after delivery." *Journal de Gynecologie, Obstetrique et Biologie de la Reproduction*. 1995, 119–126.

6. Farrel, Dave. "The Impossible Choice." *Woman's Day*. June 6, 1995, p. 87.

7. Evans, M. et. al. "Efficacy of transabdominal multifetal pregnancy reduction: collaborative experience among the world's largest centers." *Obstetrics and Gynecology*. July 1993, 61–66.

8. Seligmann, Jean and Karen Springen, "Fewer Bundles of Pain," *Newsweek*. March 4, 1996, p. 63.

9. "First Baby Born of Frozen Embryo." *The New York Times*. April 11, 1984, p. 16.

10. Ibrahim, Youssef M., "Ethical Furor Erupts in Britain: Should Unclaimed Embryos Die?" *The New York Times*. August 1, 1996, A1.

Chapter Eight

1. The title of the Office of Technology Assessment report is *Infertility, Medical and Social Choices: Summary,* Washington, D.C.: U. S. Government Printing Office, 1988.

2. Consumer protection issues involving in vitro fertilization clinics: hearing before the Subcommittee on Regulation, Business Opportunities, and Energy of the Committee on Small Business, House of Representatives, March 9, 1989. Ron Wyden's testimony appears on pages 1–3 in the official transcript.

3. Gabriel, Trip. "High-Tech Pregnancies Test Hope's Limit." *The New York Times.* January 7, 1996, A18.

4. "Black and White Twins Born After Test-tube Mix-up." *Jet.* July 24, 1995, p. 34.

5. Elliot, Dorinda and Friso Endt. "Twins—With Two Fathers." *Newsweek.* July 3, 1995, p. 35.

6. Gleicher, Norbert. "The credibility of the profession." *Journal of Assisted Reproduction and Genetics.* November 1995, 661–662.

Chapter Nine

Quotation from Helen Krouse is part of July 8, 1996 interview.

1. From an article by Lee, Felicia R. "Infertile Couples Forge Ties Within Society of Their Own." *The New York Times.* January 9, 1996, A7.

RESOURCES

In recent years, a wealth of information has been published on infertility. Here are some resources to get you started.

Books

Brown, Lesley and Gilbert, John, with Sue Freeman. *Our Miracle Called Louise: A Parents' Story*. London: Paddington Press, distributed by Grosset & Dunlap, 1979. The story of Louise Brown's conception and birth in the words of her parents.

Canadian Royal Commission on New Reproductive Technologies. *Proceed With Care*. Ottawa: Canada Communications Group, 1993. Exhaustive two-volume report on assisted reproduction and its availability in Canada. Includes recommendations on how the government should regulate the use of assisted reproduction.

Colborn, Theo, Dianne Dumanoski, and John Peterson

Myers. *Our Stolen Future*. New York: Dutton, 1996. The book argues that synthetic hormones are reducing male fertility.

Corea, Gena. *The Mother Machine*. New York: Harper & Row, 1985. A critical look at assisted reproduction from a feminist perspective.

Harkness, Carla. *The Infertility Book: A Comprehensive Medical and Emotional Guide*. Berkeley, CA: Celestial Arts, 1995. Thorough quide to fertility treatment.

Hotz, Robert Lee. *Designs on Life*. New York: Pocket Books, 1991. By focusing on the work of several world-renowned embryologists, the book gives a fascinating look at how progress is made in infertility research. Also profiles infertile couples willing to undergo experimental procedures.

Johnston, Patricia Irwin. *Taking Charge of Infertility*. Indianapolis: Perspectives Press, 1994. A self-help guide that addresses the emotional needs of couples in fertility treatment. It is intended to help couples make decisions regarding their medical treatment, including the decision to stop.

Kolata, Gina. *The Baby Doctors*. New York: Delacorte Press, 1990. A look at the short history of fetal reduction, the physicians who developed the procedure, and the couples who have made the agonizing decision to reduce.

Liptak, Karen. *Adoption Controversies*. New York: Franklin Watts, 1993. Surrogate motherhood is among the topics that this book covers.

Robin, Peggy. *How To Be A Successful Fertility Patient*. New York: W. Morrow, 1993. Easy-to-read handbook on every medical procedure connected to fertility treatment.

Shulgold, Barbara and Lynne Sipiora. *In Search of Mother-hood* (formerly *Dear Barbara, Dear Lynne*). New York: Addison-Wesley, 1992. A collection of letters exchanged by two women struggling with infertility in the 1980s.

Articles

Bloch, Hannah, and Helen Gibson. "How to Coax New Life." *Time* special issue (The Frontiers of Medicine). Fall 1996, p. 37.

"Fertility Clinics: What Are the Odds?" *Consumer Reports.* February 1996, p. 51. This consumer guide takes a hard look at in vitro fertilization.

Kolata, Gina. "Reproductive Revolution Is Jolting Old Views." *The New York Times*. January 11, 1994, A1. Thoughtful report on egg donation and host uterus.

Lawson, Carol. "Celebrated Birth Aside, Teen-Ager is Typical Now." *The New York Times*. October 4, 1993, A18. Louise Brown at 15 years old.

"Women as Wombs: The Multinational Birth Industry." *MS*. May/June, 1991. This series of articles examines assisted reproduction from several feminist perspectives. Of special interest: "International Traffic in Reproduction" by Janice G. Raymond; "Motherhood—Reclaiming the Demon Texts" by Ann Snitow; "Decoding Reprospeak" by Robyn Rowland; and "Reflections on Law, Contracts, and the Value of Life" by Patricia J. Williams.

The New York Times issue July 27, 1978. Several stories on Louise Brown's birth, including: "Scientists Praise British Birth as Triumph," A1; "Doctors to a Baby Who Made Medical History," p. A16; "Religious Leaders Differ on Implant," A16; and "Doctors Doubt Ethics in Case of British Baby," A16.

The New York Times four-part series on assisted reproduction that ran January 7–10, 1996: "High-Tech Pregnancies Test Hope's Limit," "Egg Donations Meet a Need and Raise Ethical Questions," "Infertile Couples Forge Ties Within Society of Their Own," and "From Lives Begun in Lab, Brave New Joy." All stories begin on p. A1.

Wolfe, Linda. "And Baby Makes 3, Even If You're Gray." *The New York Times*, January 4, 1994, A15. Opinion piece strongly in support of women who choose to become pregnant after menopause with donor eggs.

Organizations

For families created through surrogate motherhood, donor sperm, and donor eggs.

The Organization of Parents Through Surrogacy
P.O. Box 213
Wheeling, IL 60090
847-394-4116
http://www.opts.com

National group with local chapters across the United States. Provides information and support to people who are experiencing infertility.

RESOLVE
1310 Broadway
Somerville, MA 02114
617-623-1156 business
617-623-0744 helpline
http://www.resolve.org

Internet Sites

Due to the changeable nature of the Internet, sites appear and disappear very quickly. These resources offered useful information on infertility in general and infertility treatments at the time of publication.

American Society for Reproductive Medicine.
http://www.asrm.com

The Center for Surrogate Parenting and Egg Donation, Inc. site has information on traditional surrogate mothers as well as host uterus.
http://www.surroparenting.com

Fertilitext, an informative site with articles written by leading fertility specialists.
http://www.fertilitext.org

Many of the leading fertility clinics in the United States have Web sites that have up-to-the-minute information about assisted reproduction. Here are a few such sites:

Atlanta Reproductive Health Centre
http://www.ivf.com

Genetics & IVF Institute
http://www.givf.com

Jones Institute for Reproductive Medicine
http://www.evms.edu/jones/

INDEX

GIFT (gamete intrafallopian transfer), 79–80, 81, 109, 113, 125

Handyside, Alan, 82, 87–88, 89
Hormones, 12, 18–19, 37, 72
  abnormal levels, 23, 27, 46–47
Host uterus, 14, 48, 89–94, *91*, 97, 101–103
ICSI (Intracytoplasmic sperm injection), 50, 84–86
Immune system dysfunction, 29–30, 52
Implantation, *17*, 18, 21, 77, 82–87
Impotence, 26, 28
Infertility, defining, 15
Insurance, 13, 44, 68–69
Intercourse, timing, 18, 29, 38
Intrauterine insemination, *25*, 48, 50, 51, 52
IVF (in vitro fertilization), 11–12, 13, 14, 24, 43, 45, 47, 48, 50, 52, 64–67. *See also* Donor eggs; Multiple births
  and criticism, 59, 62–64
  history of, 55–62, *56*
  how it works, 70–79
  insurance, 68–69

micromanipulation, 82–87
success rates, 78, 81
uses, 69–70

Johnston, Patricia Irwin, 31
Jones, Howard and Georgeanna, 64, 121, 127

Laparoscopy, 39–41, *40*, 58
Male infertility, 12, 26–28, 29–31, 49–51, 52
Menopause, 21, 97
  post-menopausal pregnancy, 103–104
  premature, 23, 47, 90
Menstrual cycle, 17–18, 21, 26, 29, 37
Micromanipulation, 82–87
Microsurgery. *See* Micromanipulation
Miscarriage, 16, 23, 30, 47, 78
Multiple births, 13, 46, 72, 78–79, 83–84, 105–113, *107*
  preventing, 113–118
Myths, 32–33

OTA (Office of Technology Assessment), 122–123
Ovaries, 17–18, *17*, 20–21, 46, 71–73
Ovulation, *17*, 18, 20, 21, 23, 26, 29, 37, 45–46

Trounson, Alan, 82, 87, 89, 114, 127

Unexplained infertility, 16, 30, 41, 52
Uterine disorders, 26, 48
Uterus, 11, 14, *17*, 18–19, 20, 23, 25–26, *25*, 39. *See also* Endometriosis; Host uterus

Variocele, 28, 51
Vasectomy, 28, 51

Wapner, Ronald J., 111–112
Weight, and ovulation, 21

ZIFT (zygote intrafallopian transfer), 80–81
Zona pellucida, 19, 83

ABOUT

THE

AUTHOR

Elizabeth L. Marshall was born in Minneapolis, Minnesota, but grew up in southern California and New York City suburbs. She graduated from the University of Virginia with a B.A. in English and from the University of Pittsburgh with a M.F.A. in fiction writing. Ms. Marshall has been on the staff of *McCall's* magazine, the *Amherst Bulletin*, and *The Scientist*. She is a member of the National Association of Science Writers. Her first book, *The Human Genome Project: Cracking the Code within Us*, was published by Franklin Watts in 1996. Ms. Marshall and her husband, Jeff Seiken, now live in Columbus, Ohio, with their two young daughters.